T0064160

# Age of Brooding

Early Life and Times of Robin Blessed
- Part Four

ROBIN P. BLESSED

PARTRIDGE
A Penguin Random House Company

Copyright © 2014 by Robin P. Blessed.

ISBN:      Hardcover      978-1-4828-9555-1
           Softcover      978-1-4828-9554-4
           eBook          978-1-4828-9237-6

All rights reserved. No part of this book may be used or reproduced by any means, graphic, electronic, or mechanical, including photocopying, recording, taping or by any information storage retrieval system without the written permission of the publisher except in the case of brief quotations embodied in critical articles and reviews.

Because of the dynamic nature of the Internet, any web addresses or links contained in this book may have changed since publication and may no longer be valid. The views expressed in this work are solely those of the author and do not necessarily reflect the views of the publisher, and the publisher hereby disclaims any responsibility for them.

Scripture taken from the King James Version of the Bible.

**To order additional copies of this book, contact**
Toll Free 800 101 2657 (Singapore)
Toll Free 1 800 81 7340 (Malaysia)
orders.singapore@partridgepublishing.com

www.partridgepublishing.com/singapore

# Contents

# About Readers

R eaders are ALWAYS a special people. They are willing to set aside time to read the book they have chosen, amidst the busy daily life of family, business, and leisure.

Reading to know the author as a person who openly shares of his past—common human deeds, innermost thoughts, and deepest feelings—and as a friend willing to understand the substance of his *written voice* makes writing most rewarding. Wren and Bacon had come close in expressing my thoughts.

*Choose an author as you choose a friend.*
—Christopher Wren

*Some books are to be tasted, others to be swallowed, and some few to be chewed and digested.*
—Francis Bacon.

*A good book holds as in a vial, the purest efficacy and instruction of the living intellect that bred it.*
—Anonymous

# What Readers Say . . . About

## 'AGE OF DISCOVERY'

'Age of Discovery' is a cohesive yet progressive development to the preceding 'Age of Innocence', and draws attention to the events and experiences that shaped the author's life. Acknowledging God's footprint and blueprint in every aspect of his life, he illustrates how God looks at the people of the world. He brings to mind God's dealings with the two categories of people that make up the populace: The Wheat and The Chaff. An interesting and edifying read for sure.

—*S.M. Vijayaratnam*, Parent, Senior Manager.

Once again, Age of Discovery continues its thread faithfully from Age of Innocence, and serves out its purpose of revealing Christ through an unbeliever's life. It should help readers notice God's invisible but sure hand in their lives. It presents the case that while in vigorously attempting to deny God's existence, we very often end up 'kicking against the pricks' in unprofitable rebellion.

—*Cedric Tan,* Parent, Manager.

# What Readers Say . . . About

## 'AGE OF INNOCENCE'

I have enjoyed your book tremendously. It had helped me to begin to appreciate the events in my own life. It is a book with deep and meaningful thoughts . . . a very unique book.

—*Wu Wanjin*, Educator.

God's hand is in all that happens and the book reminds us how His righteousness prevails. Robin is able to relay his story without hints of bitterness or anger, of haughtiness or pride. The writing style is direct, concise, clear, and relevant . . . without attempts to overdrive emotions yet with just the right precision to describe the intention . . . and space enough for those moments to hold back lumps in the throat.

The writing approach is uncommon in that Robin shows even as a 'natural' man he had yearned and search for his beginnings. Now, spiritually enlightened he is able to see that God was there all the time guiding the way . . . throughout his early life, and at the end it marvels me that the Lord Jesus stands glorified still in all the years that Robin had ignored Him. I hope for more of such biographies to become useful as tools to bring out the goodness of our Lord both to unbelievers and to fellow believers.

—*Cedric Tan*, Parent, Manager.

The book brought back many fond memories of my life at the age of innocence. Truly, "to everything there is a season, and a time to every purpose under the heaven". God makes each of us different and gives us just as varied experiences in life with people, incidents, and things around us; though we may not acknowledge God's existence then.

All things that happened in life, for good or bad, joyous or sorrowful, all were just transient and eventually came to pass and became part of our memory to be aware and by reflecting, to improve and consciously change what we can. Without awareness we are overwhelmed, drowned in self-pity and be unfruitful. Since knowing Christ, memories and reflection redirected my spirit to that of thanksgiving, of thankfulness, of gratitude to God for His longsuffering, goodness, grace and mercy upon even one lost soul such as me.

The author has likewise put together pieces of fond memories in his early life for a purpose: in praise and thanksgiving to the Creator, Saviour, and Lord in his life, and through sharing it that many may come to know this great love of God. *For all this I considered in my heart even to declare all this that the righteous, and the wise, and their works, are in the hand of God: no man knoweth either love or hatred by all that is before them.*—Ecclesiastes 9:1. May the glory and love of God shine upon the heart of every reader and be blessed.

—*Samantha Quau*,
Parent, Homemaker, Home-school Educator.

An interesting book to read . . . In its use of simple flashback in time, many fond nostalgic familiar glimpses of my own journey during the age of innocence came to the fore for reflection. Throughout, the book highlights the importance of acknowledging God and having a personal relationship with Him, who is the very centre of our lives.

—*S.M. Vijayaratnam*, Parent, Senior Manager.

I enjoyed the Age of Innocence very much. I appreciate the author's reflections of his childhood—the past is not simply a distant collective memory of irreversible events, happenings and acts (and perhaps, omissions). A careful examination of childhood has shown the imprint of God's presence and provision. The past has its purpose, a purpose rooted in the source of the purpose who is the giver of life. I find myself reminded of a line in Shakespeare's *The Tempest*—"What's past is Prologue." Indeed, the past has, and will have, an undeniable role in the making of our current present and our future. God is the master weaver, and what an amazing tapestry we will see in the life of the author. This book faithfully reproduces the author's discovery of God's blessings throughout the earliest years of his life. Truly, God loads us with benefits, daily, from our beginning. Childhood can be full of richness. I am inspired. And I look forward to the Prologue that is to come.

—*April Mak*, Solicitor.


It is a book worthy of an afternoon curled up on the couch to look back in time: to reflect on what God and our parents have done for us, at the same time to count our many blessings.

—*Zhang Meifen,* Medical Practitioner.

# ABOUT THIS BOOK

*Regions of sorrow, doleful shades, where peace*
*And rest can never dwell; hope never comes,*
*That comes to all—but torture without end.*
—John Milton

This book accounts for the author's conversion at the end of his National Service stint up to five years later, when he married and went on to raise a family. As such, it is significantly for the reading benefit of Christians and contains Christian terms that may not render them familiar to the world at large. Readers may view it as the experiences of a young Christian who had to deal with the commitment to follow Christ in the light of some known and many unknown challenges, to address the expectations of a Christian; issues inherent in the church, the need to mature in the Word of God, and in the walk with God. The Scriptural quotations are from the King James Version of the Holy Bible truly the most accurate translation from the original languages, verily the very inspired Word of God.

I n the early days of my Christian life, still a 'babe' drinking only of the milk of God's word, an unscathed untried warrior for the Lord, and seeking to grow a relationship with the Master, I sought solemnly for answers to the many nagging questions in times of difficulties such as, "Is mine hope in Christ, the hope of the hypocrite who had embraced and been influenced by modern Western education?" "Is it a hope that will thus make me ashamed, having rejected and left the Buddhist faith of my family?" or "Is it a good hope through grace instead of doing good works that had been embedded in much of my life from the Buddhist upbringing?" Am I one of the many victims of self-deception? Is my profession of faith in Christ a lie or a truth? These were often re-examined in the troubling moments of deep spiritual conflicts, often setting on edge faith and disbelief, assurance and doubt. When you consider for a moment that I had always viewed my beginning and my ending as fundamental to my existence, it becomes clear that eternity was at stake upon these questions. It is heaven or hell that depends upon it. With a 'make or break' motive to examination—close, anxious, honest examination—how earnest, prayerful, and solicitous we should be, not to merely persuade ourselves or frivolously presume that we are true Christians but to see and know if we truly are. I did not follow Christ to fall into the dark pit of hell. I followed Christ to want out of this insidious darkness into the light, from the mental whims of *karma* into the arms of a definite heaven. Yet, as Milton contemplated, the Age of Brooding was for me, as *'regions of sorrow, doleful shades'*; not of gloom, for my salvation was sure, following Christ was certain; the experience was unconventionally different, to some extent unexpected; scary simply because it rested on faith, anchored in Christ. Faith is a tough call. It is as a walk into the unknown, as driving through pitch dark woods on the promise that His grace is all-sufficient. It was to venture all our eternal hope on Jesus as the Way, the Truth, and the Life. The promises of God are future in their fulfilment yet as setting them before us as present realities in our daily living in Christ; the evidence of them not factually or materially affirmed. *Now faith is the substance of things hoped for, the evidence of things not seen.*—Hebrews 11:1. This is unconventional for one steeped in the practice of cause and effect, particularly immediate or predictable visible effect. *Now the God of hope fill you with all joy and peace in believing, that ye may abound in hope, through the power of the Holy Ghost.*—Romans 15:13.

The reasoning with Christ though completed and sure, and settled to allow us to begin following Him on the journey of testing, not as in the infliction of suffering but in tests to deepen and strengthen our faith to progress our continuance on that journey, gaining confidence, that is, faith in the trustworthiness of our Leader. He sits as the refiner that we may come forth as gold. At the first repentance of sin in our lives—both original sin in our human nature, and our very own sins in the conduct of life—we accepted that Christ had redeemed us from that bondage and enslavement of sin when he died on the cross and rose the third day. Yet, this very foundation of faith in Christ for our salvation remained continually challenged in the face of waking ticking reality in the world of darkness. Up until this first repentance, we had never repented; we may have only regretted relative to the circumstance surrounding sin. We have never truly felt sorry, for we did not seek to remorsefully and vehemently turn from that sinful nature and look to Christ for salvation. Only when we have repented of our sinful nature, turning from it in abandonment, God seeing in our penitent heart, a contrite spirit regenerates us, applying to us the benefits of Christ's atonement. The life-giving Spirit gives us a new life in the new birth. Afterwards, the devil stands at the door ever ready to incessantly assail us with thoughts of the impossibility of salvation due to our total depravity, and to accuse our regenerate lives of their sinful past. He is never at rest in battering the gates of our early faith, always casting seeds of doubt upon the fallowed earth of our ready hearts, incessantly mocking our adversities, ever ready to rain eggs of derision at every stumble we make. Let us all, under the influence of these thoughts, carry to our merciful God the prayer of the Psalmist, "*Search me, O God, and know my heart; try me, and know my thoughts and see if there be any wicked way in me and lead me in the way everlasting.*" These words were often on many young Christians' lips, as a means of averting the darts of hurt. However, it is only when we wear them on our hearts, that we will emerge victorious. Pray as the psalmist did, that they have their due effect upon our daily walk and life in Christ. These incessant accusations, doubts, and conflicts cast our way offer us the necessary tests of our fitness for the Potter's use. They are the devil's means to shaken our faith in the blood of Christ, to rock any semblance of assurance in the everlasting Hope, and tear us from the worship of our God. Time and experience—in trials and in afflictions—converge to enable us to cling on in faith to an interest in Christ, and see God in His appointed moments of truth.

Brooding is real in our Christian walk as we ponder on the issues of life as in the bird warming its eggs, or as we are in the test crucible laid over a flame to draw forth the elements from the composite through the heat of the fire that distinguishes and separates. It is as though not one Christian is spared the maturing process—the 'mandatory' natural time of brooding—to break out of the shell prematurely was never in God's plan. Salvation is sure; what we needed was the faith and courage to go forth until such a time as God sees fit to move His hand to reveal in His appointed time, the goodness of His Providence. We may traverse a parched barren land only to finally reach lush verdant pastures that were all worth the sojourn. God intends for each of His children to be fully fit for His Kingdom, not by our works in our own human wisdom but by faith in Him in obedient and willing conviction to His righteousness just as Christ, the Son of God was obedient to the Father's will and bidding. God provides the resources and the means to take us to the destination. We cannot do anything to please God out of our sinful nature, only Christ's redemptive work in us as we look to Him for deliverance, and our willingness to be led by the unction of the Holy Spirit, will produce the fruit pleasing to God. He asks only that we go forward and upward in faith, resting on His promises, on His changeless righteousness. God the Father, God the Son, and God the Holy Spirit, all three work together in perfect union to prepare us for His Kingdom.

David Livingstone caught the fearless spirit of our Master, of our Lord Jesus Christ, when he penned this powerful line in his diary, ill and far away from any friend, and abandoned by his medicine-carrier. *"I am immortal till my work is done."* May we in like manner be fearless and heed only His call of "Follow Me," to move forward in faith on our Christian journey. That which He had begun, He shall complete and perfect. What is there to fear when even a sparrow shall not fall without our Father's assent? To 'follow' takes a moment's decision. On the road, that decision tested for self-denial and self-sacrifice still had to stand up against buffetings from derision, doubt, shame, guilt, fear, and reverses.

I urge my readers to note well that the age of brooding will be with us in our Christian sojourn on earth. By following Christ and brooding over His mystery, we may deepen our love and knowledge of Him and things spiritual. By God's appointment, you may miss it; if you do not, take heed then to be sure, His grace is sufficient for you to ride it out. Learn from it; for the gems of Christ's beauty and glory lay before us in every circumstance, for the picking; His promises made and given, all ready for the discovery and the rendering. Remember, He is our Master and Teacher. He knows all, He sees all, and He cares for all. He loves all without end.

Look to Him in faith and trust Him completely to answer that faith. Come to Christ that you may enter into our heavenly Father's presence as adopted children in Him, as heirs with Him. Walk in Christ, walk in His Way in humility and obedience, and in faith for the saving grace; that you may know He is the Truth and to find your life in His Life. Christ's Way is the way to heaven, and the way to life everlasting.

# INTRODUCTION

*This I recall to my mind, therefore have I hope.*
*It is of the LORD'S mercies that we are not consumed, because*
*his compassions fail not.*
*They are new every morning: great is thy faithfulness.*
*The LORD is my portion, saith my soul; therefore will I hope in*
*him.*
*The LORD is good unto them that wait for him, to the soul that*
*seeketh him.*
*It is good that a man should both hope and quietly wait for the*
*salvation of the LORD.*
*—Lamentations 3:21-26.*

This introduction to the book explains the idea of 'brooding' thus lending an idea as to the title of the book. Brooding reflects the believer's challenging attempt to bridge the beliefs and tenets he has embraced to answer the realities and issues that he faces, and will face in the functioning of life.

Brooding, as we all understand it, means sitting on, covering, and warming, as a fowl on her eggs for the purpose of warming them and hatching chickens, or as a hen over her chickens, to warm and protect them.

Another understanding is that of dwelling on with anxiety, to remain a long time in anxiety or solicitous thought; to have the mind uninterruptedly dwell a long time on a subject, as the miser broods over his gold.

In a sense, brooding is maturing something or anything with care, where maturing is much like dwelling solicitously over a matter, a subject under consideration, be it the eggs and/or newly hatched chicks, or in the author's case, his engagement in the Christian faith, when he followed Jesus Christ. With that decision to follow Jesus, he chose to live his life in Jesus and subject himself to the will of God, his heavenly Father. Christ in His Person was central in his faith. His only conviction was his belief in Christ—the very nature of Christ as revealed through the gospels—and His obedience as the only acceptable sacrifice to propitiate for the sins of the world and thereby justify (to make just and right) a just God's wrath (or justice) on an unjust world. The love and mercy of God to us in our sin and misery convince and lead us to repentance. Thus enlightened, we may embrace Christ's payment by His death on the cross as our redemption from the bondage of sin (eternal death), and adoption into God's kingdom. We, who once walked in darkness, now walk in the light. *For by grace are ye saved through faith; and that not of yourselves: it is the gift of God:*—Ephesians 2:8

With that conviction and the follow-on commitment, the author took upon himself the unknown relationship challenges from all those about him—his parents, less of his siblings, his relatives, and friends—and in the *possible* prodigal waste of time, in such a sudden and inconceivable endeavour. *So likewise, whosoever he be of you that forsaketh not all that he hath, he cannot be my disciple.*—Luke 14:33.

The Christian life implies suffering and endurance. It is in the bearing of pain, affliction, constraint, temptation, restraint, distress, persecution, wrong, or hardship—that patience is developed. *And not only so, but we glory in tribulations also: knowing that tribulation worketh patience; and patience, experience; and experience, hope*—Romans 5:3-4. *But if we hope for that we see not, then do we with patience wait for it.*—Romans 8:25. *For whatsoever things were written aforetime were written for our learning, that we through patience and comfort of the scriptures might have hope*—Romans 15:4. Patience is the character or habit of mind that enables us to suffer afflictions, calamities, provocations, or other evils—with a calm, unruffled temper; endurance without murmur or fret, in calmness, in composure. Tribulations cultivate and reap patience, which in turn offers experience that flourishes and brightens the hope of our assurance in following Christ. We are God's fallowed ground, for the seeding of His love and mercy; and in due season, of reaping His privileges and benefits in Christ. *Now the God of patience and consolation grant you to be likeminded one toward another according to Christ Jesus.*—Romans 15:5. *Now the God of peace be with you all. Amen.*—Romans 15:33.

The narrow or strait gate is the self-abandonment and self-accusation that are indispensable for entrance into salvation, with which we must reckon. The door of faith is a narrow one that will not let in bloated self-righteousness, inflated worldly glories, and exalted loud dignities. We stay out until we strip ourselves of bejewelled kingly crowns and rich royal vestures, and stand clothed only in the bare and naked skin of penitence. We must make ourselves tiny to get in; our self-righteousness, glories, and dignities dressed us larger than the strait gate would allow. Even in the skin of our guilt and shame, we must curl up or prone, creep, and crawl on all fours, to constrain ourselves to its lowly frame; we must leave absolutely everything outside; so restrictively narrow is it. We must go in one by one, as in the turnstiles at the gates of a football stadium. The door opens into a palace, but it is too strait for anyone who trusts to himself. We must exert effort in order to enter by it. For everything in our old self-confident, self-centred nature is innately ingrained to be, and is up in arms against the conditions of entrance. Our salvation is not by blemished human effort, but we shall not yet believe without effort. The main struggle of our whole lives should be to cultivate meek and self-humbling trust in Jesus Christ, and to fight the good fight of faith. *Then said one unto him, Lord, are there few that be saved? And he said unto them, strive to enter in at the strait gate: for many, I say unto you, will seek to enter in, and shall not be able.*—Luke 13:23-24.

Just a thought here may quicken our understanding of the meek and lowly Person of Christ, the Son of God. God in His love for the world gave us the Christ, who in complete obedience to the Father's will left all in heaven, to come as man to secure everlasting life for whosoever believes in Him by faith. He rises from His royal seat on the right hand of God, to lower Himself from it to be as a servant, removes His kingly robes to surrender and disown His rights of royalty, unbuckles His glorious girdle to complete His disrobement, and loosens His vestures for the rags of earth. Of a virgin birth, to chosen righteous and humble parents in swaddling clothes in a lowly manger, He grew in the spirit of the Word of God, laboured as the common man, all to the honour and glory of God. He had nowhere to lay his head while the foxes have holes. He grew in stature and wisdom before God and man.

The age of brooding for the author was a period of questioning about the religious faith he had clung to after having met his Master and Saviour, the Lord Jesus Christ, not as in a first person physical encounter yet as good as one. Jesus was completely coherent in His life as recorded in the four Gospels he read, perfectly in concord, not tainted as a conspicuous dot on a clean white sheet or cast as an iota of oddity on the scripture of absolute congruence. He was in perfect unity with the four Gospels of the Bible. The questioning for the author was not one of doubt about Christ; he was sure of Christ. It was about his attempt to align his faith in Christ to the reality of the Christian and secular worlds, a seemingly peculiar effort at reconciling a Christian world still in the shadows of darkness and a secular world still in total darkness. A Christian yet to be perfected may appear to catch a glimpse of the Light, not all of it. There was work still undone; we are as unfinished products, Christians that are still a work in progress.

At the meeting with Jesus, perfect in manner, the author was clear in the understanding of his sinful nature, as he repented over them, and turned away from them, and believed in Jesus for his salvation. Next, he had to consider the manner to follow Jesus, the need to work out his belief, and to work out his salvation. The author's belief was not a passive one, but one totally compelled by the very perfect nature of the Son of God. Jesus died for him as for the rest of the world who are unquestionably, undeserving for God's sacrifice of His own Son to redeem man from God's wrath and from the bondage of sin. He waited not for any to tell him how to work out his salvation. Christ had said "Follow Me," and that to him was all-sufficient. His cue was Christ. His follow-on actions were all that Christ had done: tell all they have sinned and therefore are eternally damned; tell all that Christ is the Son of God and He saves; tell all that they are reconciled to and therefore at peace with God by Christ's death on the cross. Tell all that whosoever believes in Christ has overcome death; they *should not perish but have everlasting life.*

*Verily, verily, I say unto you, except a corn of wheat fall into the ground and die, it abideth alone: but if it die, it bringeth forth much fruit. He that loveth his life shall lose it; and he that hateth his life in this world shall keep it unto life eternal. If any man serve me, let him follow me; and where I am, there shall also my servant be: if any man serve me, him will my Father honour.—* John 12:24-26.

# APPROACH TO THIS BOOK

*Remember not the sins of my youth, nor my transgressions:*
*according to thy mercy remember thou me for thy goodness' sake,*
*O LORD. Good and upright is the LORD: therefore will he*
*teach sinners in the way. The meek will he guide in judgment:*
*and the meek will he teach his way. All the paths of the LORD*
*are mercy and truth unto such as keep his covenant and his*
*testimonies.*
—Psalms 25:7-10.

'Approach to this book' offers an overview of the contents of the book, rendering them to synchronise with the sequence of the book's chapters. The chapters ease into each other in a practical and chronological sequence, and are welded together seamlessly, some by aid of **Notes** at the end of certain chapters in an attempt to remove the clutter of details from the main theme.

Throughout this book, the author purposed to write of the pivotal situations he encountered then as he sought to discover and grasp the Christian faith that he committed to with unquestioned assurance. He would then share thoughts as questions or as contemplations at that time in separate chapters to explore his understanding and perspective as they now stand. You may think of it as personal interpretation in the light of what the Scripture reveals to us. It may have taken some decades of his life but at the end, it was sure, his salvation was sure, his faith was sure, his hope not misplaced; *morning by morning, new mercies I see, great is God's faithfulness.* We must be faithful till we come to the place of rest in Christ Jesus. That place is where we can go to, to claim the resources Jesus has available for us, to claim of His resourcefulness. For we have nothing when we come to draw from His largesse that our Father in heaven had given Him in His obedience and steadfastness as the Son of man, and in His person as God the Son. We have precious promises of the gospel at our disposal. When Christ went to the cross to redeem us in His blood, all-sufficient to propitiate for our sins and the sins of the world, our pardons were sealed eternally. *My little children, these things write I unto you, that ye sin not. And if any man sin, we have an advocate with the Father, Jesus Christ the righteous: And he is the propitiation for our sins: and not for ours only, but also for the sins of the whole world.*—1 John 2:1-2; by which He also reconciled us to God. *For if, when we were enemies, we were reconciled to God by the death of his Son, much more, being reconciled, we shall be saved by his life.*—Romans 5:10.

Christ's resurrection by the Holy Spirit shall also quicken our mortal bodies by His Spirit that dwells in us. *But if the Spirit of him that raised up Jesus from the dead dwell in you, he that raised up Christ from the dead shall also quicken your mortal bodies by his Spirit that dwelleth in you.*—Romans 8:11.

The sequence of the author's pivotal experiences from the time of his conversion after leaving National Service to the time of his twenty-sixth year when he married, have been reported in chronological order as closely as possible. Where overlaps occur as a result of referencing to related incidents and/or thoughts, the author would explain them as is necessary. What follows below are summaries about each chapter or a group of chapters to thread them sequentially in time; incidentally, they offer also the logical order as of stepping stones in his early Christian life.

**Follow Me!** From **National Service into the world of work** was a transition from two and a half years of involuntary 'cloistered' space and time, and into the necessarily practical world of work, when the veil removed and uncertainties entered. The challenge was that of making out on one's own, not with the equipage of weapons to tackle all the *unknown* issues that would come along. The *known's* and *given's* were that he was not going to university, he did not have a trade he specialised in save the yet-to-complete accounting diploma with which he had no interest; he was penniless and without support but for the family's moral encouragement. Things got worse when he followed Jesus Christ; that summarily and literally ended the father-son relationship between Pa and him. He was in limbo and 'alone'. Christ was all he had. His lot was cast, his portion assigned. He had one path to take; there was none else from which to choose.

**Conversion to Christianity** announced the end of earthly son-ship with Pa and the heavenly adoption in Christ. His life search for the purpose of his being and existence ended when he knew where he came from and where he would head to, how it was all possible because of the grace of God, of His love and mercy; and through faith in Christ and His redemptive work at the cross for all mankind. The author was dead in sin, now regenerate, raised in Christ to newness of life. He has a change of mind to follow all of Christ and turn from his wayward life. *He is transformed a new creature in Christ, to not conform to the world.* (Romans 12:2)

Now his search for meaning in the Christian life began. He was on another journey, a new one, an unfamiliar one torn between the old person and the new by faith in Christ Jesus. Following Christ did not come as a clean break from the past and the old. Vestiges hung about in every corner of his life as cobwebs that refuse to detach and be scattered. How can one, by any serious effort, overcome and be rid of them?

The first thing he thought about was to look for and join a **church.** Was that a perception from the past, an expectation in Christianity? We expect Christians to go to church. That was what he had always known. Was it the urging of the Holy Spirit that prompted him to want to go to church? Surely, it must be the latter, having a new birth, infused with the breath and Spirit of God to live in His bidding, to be with other like-minded brethren in Christ. There was a desire to belong among fellow saints.

To **which church** should he go? Starting out with a new found faith, re-born or regenerated in the Holy Spirit, he was in spirit counselled to look for a church, a place where he could fellowship and meet with others of the same faith, to be encouraged and to seek opportunities to grow and mature in his conduct and walk as a Christian. It would be hazardous to be in a world of contrary kinship, without first having a sound and solid grounding in the doctrines of Christianity, in the teachings of Christ. The Word was the basis and to him the church embodied the place for deeper collective study of God's word, the fellowship of believers, where corporate opportunities exist to sow the message of the gospel of Christ, and harvest from a rich field of the lost to bring in to Christ. Yet that first church to which he went was a charismatic church seemingly suited to his young Christian mind; it was where he was baptised by water immersion, received church membership, and served in various ministries. He found it in the classified advertisement of the local newspapers. That first church was also his first committed exposure to a community of fellow believers, charismatic Christians, seemingly not fully aligned to other supposedly mainstream orthodox denominations such as Roman Catholic, and Protestant that included Methodist, Anglican, Presbyterian, Lutheran, and so on. Charismatic churches included the Assembly of God (AOG) and Pentecostals; they believed in baptism of the Holy Spirit, speaking in tongues, and healing. They were hyper-friendly people smiling and with hugely positive 'praise-the-Lord' utterances in all matters good or bad; they raised, waved, and clapped their hands in singing along with mildly rhythmic, lively, and catchy music in accompaniment. Songs were lyrically contemporary interspersed with a few traditional hymns sung in contemporary beat. The church he went to held their services at a hotel auditorium large enough for its worshippers for it did not have a permanent building of its own.

This church took a bit of getting used to but he evidently became a part of it: in due time, he was baptised there, received into membership, and served in several capacities. For five years, he never spoke in 'tongue', it simply never happened for him; he felt himself odd, stood out as of a different feather, yet accepted for his Christian fervour. He had little understanding of all that went on. Tongue speaking, interpretation, and prophecy were gifts of the Holy Spirit; they pointed out from Scripture—one simply ask and receive them; he did, yet received not, it remained a mildly unsettling puzzle. Yet, he wondered why he should need it; the Spirit was already in him. Bible study focused on Christian living, still a lot to do with human effort that was as a list of 'How To' pointers to follow. He realised at this church, after a while, that Christ became *nominal* in Christian living. Christ was as though re-enacted during weekly worship for us to adore in a rather emotional fashion. In the circumstances his foundational roots not deeply sunk, he was as a seed sown on ground with shallow earth. He left the church at the end of five years, took a break before revisiting the church issue. There was often the danger of the *church* not having a sound, scripture-based comprehensive inductive methodology leaving new entrants Biblically weak in doctrine and fundamentals. New *entrants* without a scriptural foundation became mere inductees who, when not tended, would fall away by the wayside. If still sucking the milk of their regeneration and in following the church practices than Christ, never exercising their faith to look to the meat of the Word, they end up with a lack of conviction in following Christ to the letter and in His Spirit. The church with sound doctrine would not have left the regenerated child of God famished, anaemic, and without life. Both church and church-goers were worse off when not well directed in the Truth. The name of 'Christian' is an important one, it marked him out as belonging to Christ, as one called of God to be separate from the world for His church; as the Jewish nation was the people called of God to be separate from the heathen for His Kingdom. ***Congregating with other Christians to worship God in church on the Lord's Day is a mandate.*** Attending a scripture-based church is fundamental to starting out right in the Christian faith and growing in Christian maturity and stature.

**Doctrine** was tantamount to a serious interest and study of the Word of God. It is Bible study with a purposeful and systematic approach to a definite purpose of deeply knowing the Word. *In the beginning was the Word, and the Word was with God, and the Word was God. The same was in the beginning with God.*—John 1:1-2. Jesus Christ was the Word. God gave us the Word. Christ was the good news, the gospel. Doctrine exposes the Word of God, the basis of God's salvation plan for wayward man. Doctrine enables us to not treat Christian statements casually or superficially in assumptive vernacular language. Doctrine requires us to be more forensic, precise, and oftentimes necessarily expository. ***God's Word defines doctrine.***

**Soul winning** is a command from Jesus: *And Jesus came and spake unto them, saying, all power is given unto me in heaven and in earth. Go ye* *therefore, and teach all nations, baptizing them in the name of the Father, and of the Son, and of the Holy Ghost: Teaching them to observe all things whatsoever I have commanded you: and, lo, I am with you alway, even unto the end of the world. Amen.*—Matthew 28:20.

'Soul winning' is not a term we can find anywhere in the Bible except in Proverbs 11:30—*The fruit of the righteous is a tree of life; and he that winneth souls is wise.* The context of winning souls in the verse from Proverbs is probably different from what we understand soul winning to mean today in the context of Matthew 28:20. The idea was that the central purpose of our life was the salvation of man, and of us. We have received our salvation from eternal death and the fearful wrath of God; we were thus motivated to bring the good news of salvation to all others who still roamed the world in darkness. Having been under damnation and now lived in the light, our desire was to draw men to Christ and bring Christ to them. The author's involvement in the Youth for Christ (YFC) movement and the 3:16 Ministry, both of which were youth groups while the first Billy Graham Crusade in Singapore shared the gospel at mega rallies on a national scale, offered insights into how evangelism worked in those contexts, though not fully persuaded of the approaches employed. ***Soul winning is a command.***

**Christian living** was simply about following Christ. Our regenerated lives must produce the character of Christ. We have learned of Him, we adored Him, we were compelled to follow Him without question; we can worship and honour only Him. All our hopes and affections we have laid at His feet. All of our conversations, all of our thoughts, and the deliberations of our heart cannot deviate from the One we adored. Our deeds and walk must be in synchrony and harmony to His character, otherwise we are clearly out of step, out of 'synch'. We have such a perfect and mighty example in Christ. *The tree is known by its fruit;* ***a Christian is known by his walk, the conduct of his Christian life*** all of his days.

**Jesus Christ is the way, the truth, and the life.** After the five years at church, the author had shallow roots, he knew he was far from the journey's end and was tired; his heart was homesick for heaven. What he knew of Christ in His utterances, His walk, and His teachings, had truly been on the surface assumed at face value. He had not dug deeper to connect with other Biblical principles to make perfect sense of issues he faced as a young Christian. It was five years in serving at every ministry he possibly could lay his hands on, in earnest zeal for following Christ. It all somehow came to nought and he felt as a failure for Christ. Jesus Christ the Way, the Truth, and the Life was as a Christian motto, as part of a creed, a regular utterance that had not sunk deeply to render him strength in his still young faith. *How was Christ the Way and to what? How was Christ the Truth? What was the truth? How was Christ the Life in his life?*

He gave of his best and it was as though he had missed the mark of Christianity, and lost much in the process. He had worked diligently in his day time career in accounting, he gave unreservedly in time, effort, and financial resources to the Lord's work, his professional development not tended, and he had set aside the thought of marriage and raising a family. He was rather broken. The Lord was graciously merciful and beckoned him to "**come apart . . . and rest**." It was a loving break, as a 'retreat', a merciful gift from the Lord at the brink of personal internal turmoil. It was a much needed reprieve, a time of quiet away from corporate Christian activities, and of contemplation of all that had gone past, a time of healing, a refreshing time of waiting upon the Lord. It was a retreat of sorts. It was a time of solitude, a time to draw close to the Lord, to experience His fellowship in quietude, and the pleasures of resting under His trusting wings.

He was **out of the woods, still in the wilderness**, and the pilgrimage must continue until Christ comes again, as it was in old times, when God's salvation existed in shadows of things to come until Christ came as God-man. The author began an understanding that life's sojourn here on earth will be a continuous traverse of the terrain in the wilderness—woods, valleys, and mountains—one after another, until Christ establishes us in Him. These woods were but tests of our knowledge, understanding, and faith in the Lord Jesus Christ; these can come only through trials in those woods to 'stretch' our faith in Him in the midst of temptation, to knead us into the shape of His comeliness, to 'hammer' our wills in harmony with His. All that is required of us is the willingness to receive of His rains, and to drink from His eternal fountain of living waters as He draws us to them. We simply receive to possess of His freely flowing grace, to appropriate Him in our hearts that we may never thirst again of the Life that is in Christ.

# PROLOGUE

*A man may be a true believer, and yet would give all the world,
were it in his power, to know that he is a believer. To have
grace, and to be sure that we have grace is heaven on this side of
heaven.*
—Thomas Brooks, in Heaven on Earth

The preceding parts had dealt with the nature of this book, providing a summary introduction to the *brooding* expectations that the author would relate, and the organisation of this book. The prologue steps on all of the past and casts now a thin short line to thread the foregoing looming experiences—turbulent, bumpy, and crude—in solicitously seeking out the way, the truth, and the life; to purposefully reach the Epilogue of *this* book that spells only the end of the start of his Christian life. Till our last earthly breath is drawn, we can surely say that the end of one thing is really the beginning of another. He had started out surely and strongly for the whole stretch of the *age of brooding* with a full-blown dedication short of fanaticism. Yet at the end of it, the Lord in Fatherly love called him to come apart and rest; in quietude to mull over all that had gone before, in joys and in tears, with victories and the scars to show, and wait upon the Lord. *Now the God of hope fill you with all joy and peace in believing, that ye may abound in hope, through the power of the Holy Ghost.*—Romans 15:13

From every prologue to its epilogue, let us well remember that the Lord God Almighty had been the Master Designer in allowing all that had happened to happen, in restraining that which He willed otherwise, and therefore, providentially crafting all that came to pass and all that will come to pass.

# 1

## FOLLOW ME!
## From National Service,
## into the world of Work

*For I am the LORD, I change not;*
*therefore ye sons of Jacob are not consumed.*
—Malachi 3:6

Two and a half years away to National Service were largely in the first year like living behind high walls to keep trainees/soldiers focused on their service shut out from the prying eyes of those outside and away from loved ones who need not know about what went on in the camps. Even if they did, they can do nothing about it. National Service truly was a lesson in a ministry of some sort where commitment bore upon the serving, as the minister who was required to complete that mandated service that all young men alike had to perform. National Servicemen as far as was known, seldom talked to their loved ones about life in the camp; utterance of the secret experience was as a murmur, as betrayal of the code of manliness perhaps. Once the mystery of National Service had become less than curious after the first year, the rest of National Service was in the most part very manageable, with time to take on personal pursuits either in the evenings or on weekends.

The author had little preparation for the world other than a partial accounting qualification from the United Kingdom that would put him in good stead to enter the accounting profession either in industry or in the domain of auditing, and by furthering education in the evenings made for full qualification. His preparation was that he was not prepared to enter the accounting profession. He had no inclination for accounting, from the moment his father, Pa made the decision for him some years ago. The path seemed as though set now for him to take the accounting route or to work at entry level jobs in most industries. The range included civil service administration to lab assistants/technician roles in oil and gas/chemicals, to inventory assistants, and a whole range of 'assistant' roles. It appeared a sensible place to start to learn a trade and moved up through the ranks by study and industry. His alma mater, RI, known to nurse the nation's top civil servants, civil service came to mind naturally. He set about looking for such opportunities and they were plentiful. He went to one and had to complete the job application then and there. He received three sets of 4-page forms to fill out. Today we call them 'triplicates'. He completed the first set of forms with much stoicism; and was simply unable to bring himself to begin the next set. Triplicates were impossible let alone one set of forms. He was adamant that an applicant should not fill in extra sets of forms to meet an organisation's internal inefficiency in system or structure; it was simply meaningless. This was not what work life should be; this was not what work should be like. He tore off all the forms, threw them into the waste basket nearby, and walked out of that place with such a strong conviction not to apply for a job in an organisation that practises what he considered as inefficiencies. Such organisations do appear weak in their will, much more than in their lack of means and ability, to improve and to institute change that will benefit its people, customers, and business associates. He believed in working for and with businesses that had character or a semblance of it. This was not any different from our dealings with men in the world. We may be *in* the world and must surely not be *of* the world. That avowal of his has not wavered since. It is necessary that the reader consider the author's naïveté in all of this without matured counsel and without professional guidance.

He then turned to the commercial sector, and found the U.S. multinational companies more congenial; no triplicates, more informative about their organisations, about the positions they advertised, more human in general as they test for intelligence, articulation, skills, and aptitude; there was greater willingness to communicate. In every one of these firms, he met several of his RI schoolmates applying for the same position. It was certainly a very competitive field.

An old friend at RI who left in the fourth year there, who had kept in touch, knew he had a partial accounting qualification urged that he should not waste it but to enter the auditing field where there was a strong demand for new entrants. He decided to write in and received a call to attend an interview. He ended up as an Audit Assistant with a monthly salary of two hundred and forty dollars, somewhat worse than the National Service income. There was also a three-month probation attached.

He made past probation and received supervised assignments that would progress his development in audit through an inductive process. There were many mundane work activities meted out to entry level assistants as was typically expected to supposedly be more cost effective, as we were the lowest paid in the audit ranks. Such mundane tasks included those further described here. *Casting* was adding across and down on a spread sheet analysis to confirm the numbers balanced and therefore numerically accurate for use in the next step in the audit process. *Vouching* of a book entry to a source document that could be an invoice, voucher, purchase order, and so on that initiated the entry in the first place tested for proper recording. *Sighting* of a physical item against the supporting document or record authenticated the existence of the item entered. *Process review* showed consistent procedural flows, with the proper approval and authorisation to initiate an occurrence. The only exciting bit in audit was the independent analysis using numbers from the financial statements to classify, and explain the results from the business point of view. In the process, oftentimes certain irregularities could surface that required further audit. Analysis also helped in understanding the way a business functioned.

It was here in auditing that he met his future wife, his help meet for his earthly life. He had seen her often before and nodded in acknowledgement mostly. He got to know her better inadvertently when he received instructions to render under supervision, general supporting junior audit assistance at a major client. She was also on that team. She was petite, with an outlook quite comparable to the author's secondary-four Chinese teacher at RI—young, bright, an eager beaver, held herself up professionally, and probably less fragile than his teacher. She, a year younger than the author, and actually was at RI in her pre-university years. They have never met when they were at RI; she was in engineering. She went to a girls' Methodist school for ten years before applying for a place at RI. She received salvation from the Lord's grace and visitation when at secondary three. Sitting across each other and spending many late hours at the client's office among other colleagues offered opportunities to fellowship at close-up. The friendship blossomed and the author boldly extended an invitation to the cinema for a late night 9 p.m. movie. The movie was Cecil de Mille's 'Ten Commandments'. They had dinner after work and proceeded to the cinema. A woman and a man, both are unique individuals, each personally and directly in union with Christ. Coming together as in union between them, they are as Christ and His bride, the church. The woman relieves man of his loneliness and walks in union with him in the struggles of life as a companion, submitting to his authority. From the man she receives love, protection, and care. Together they worship God.

He left auditing after about nine months at it, feeling a need to deepen his knowledge by actually keeping a full set of the accounting books for a business firm in industry. It would give him access to understanding the dynamics of operations in a business, and relate them to financial accounting. In short, he wanted in on the thick of the action so he could figure out for himself all that he was doing. It was as returning to first principles for a strong grasp of finance and accounting. He applied for a position in a branch office of a U.S. MNC specialising in the sale and reconditioning of flow control valves that served the marine, oil and gas industries. That change of job landed him a salary increase of just under twenty per cent of his last salary at audit. He made past probation and the annual reviews. He grew in his work responsibilities, received a pleasant surprise by way of a major senior assignment from the managing director when his department manager was on vacation. With much effort due to ignorance and inexperience, he read up the subject and pulled through the assignment, meeting expectations. After a year and a half, he wanted to do more and applied to a U.S. MNC that manufactured engine lathes used in precision steel cutting processes. Another significant salary increase helped his career progress, and his diligence, inquisitiveness, willingness to do more, effective articulation and communication, and a pleasant personality won the hearts of his peers and seniors. Once again, he wanted to do more and went on to another U.S. MNC in oil and gas engineering services. He performed well in several major projects and received promotion to a full-fledged accountant. Two years there and he moved within the company to a project control engineering role that still made use of his accounting specialisation and budgetary skills. In this role, he learnt a great deal about the business side of things. Work was certainly enormously enjoyable for him as he was able to plan and compress all the mundane routine activities in order that he could use the time created to explore operational opportunities. That made him deeply knowledgeable and enthusiastic at his tasks bearing favourably upon his exemplary performance. He continued with self-study in the evenings to complete his accounting certification. All in all, the Lord was with him, blessing him and providentially directing his path. He walked *in* the Lord, in faith; for the Lord was faithful. One may feel disinclination to accounting and for that matter to anything, yet when trusting in the Lord the author learns that it is not at the object that we lay our eyes but rather in Christ's way that we dutifully lay our minds, our hearts, and our hands.

Work for things eternal: they are easy, light, and restful.
*Come unto me, all ye that labour and are heavy laden, and I will give you rest. Take my yoke upon you, and learn of me; for I am meek and lowly in heart: and ye shall find rest unto your souls. For my yoke is easy, and my burden is light.*—Matthew 11:28-30. Knowing that work in the world—strenuous, heavy laden, and overbearing—for things of sustenance in the world, is really our portion in life, our Christian duty for the love, praise, and honour of Christ. As we look to the eternal, let us be mindful that we walk and work in a temporal and imperfect world; we can accept our portion with gratitude and with joy, knowing full well we are children of God, and that in the name of Christ Jesus we have full access to our heavenly Father's power, honour, and glory. We have the benefits and privileges as sons of God. Our freedom from the wrath of God's displeasure (with our sin) had been sealed by Christ's redemptive work on the cross. Christ had borne all at Calvary in His meekness and lowliness, in His Way; take His yoke upon us for it is easy and the burden is light.

# 2

## ADOPTED in Christ; DISOWNED by his own.

*And we have known and believed the love that God hath to us.
God is love; and he that dwelleth in love dwelleth in God, and
God in him. Herein is our love made perfect, that we may have
boldness in the day of judgment: because as he is, so are we in
this world. There is no fear in love; but perfect love casteth out
fear: because fear hath torment. He that feareth is not made
perfect in love. We love him, because he first loved us.*
—1 John 4:16-19.

*He came unto his own, and his own received him not.
But as many as received him, to them gave he power to become
the sons of God, even to them that believe on his name.*
—John 1:11, 12.

One evening after dinner, the author broke the news of his conversion, of his following Jesus Christ, of becoming a Christian, and leaving all his past Buddhist beliefs and glories in the dust. He had brooded over how to break the news many days before, and had thought about possible outcomes from anger to violence. Finally, he had to do it, the lots cast whatever hell may let loose; he prepared for the worst for he trusted in Christ. So it was.

His father Pa flew into a burning rage wishing he could strike sense into his own son: a rage not seen before, as one fighting for his life, knocking over every reason and every compromise that stood in his way. Pa would have torn his son into shreds had the author not been his son. From since his youth, Pa was the author's highest estimation of a hero, his beloved father, someone he had looked up to; yet now, he felt sorry for Pa who did not have the precious promises of Christ. He had prayed that the Lord would light gently on Pa and convert him. He felt a great anguish that Pa was not Christian. Pa was a deeply devoted person but to the wrong god. Pa had always put his hopes in his oldest boy, he had always been proud of him as a son, obedient and diligent, who never failed to honour his father in all endeavours. He was as Pa's favoured son.

In the author's revelation of a complete turnabout, Pa's tall towers began to crumble, the walls cracked up, the hopes, and dreams of a proud father totally and absolutely pulverised. It was deeply inconceivable, unreasonably impossible, beyond all sense of the rational. The author could feel Pa's deep sorrow as having lost a son to the jaws of death; it put a nail to Pa's heart, and tore Pa in rage and left the author speechless and in seeming helplessness. Pa was decisive; he shouted in delirium, punched the table to release his torment, marched into his room, and slammed the door so hard that the wooden doorposts rattled and loosened themselves from the sides cemented to the adjacent walls. Pa had gone into his room to be by himself, to commiserate with silence, to cry out his pain that no one would ever witness, not even his wife, Mie. His pride was completely in the dust; years of the sense of parenting success dissipated as wisps of smoke without trace. There was nothing left for him to grasp, not even straws. He withdrew into himself, into his tired shrunken heart, deflated and inelastic, bearing not an ounce of desire to revive and recover. He could do nothing; he could not beg his son to turn around his decision nor could he force him. It was as though he hung on too long to a slowly losing bet, and now that bet was lost forever.

The whole house fell quiet, not a sound of anyone shifting, everyone stood in his/her place nearly motionless, and looking at each other and at the author, to feel and fathom the depth of the anguish that he had brought to bear in the household. There was no forward warning; it came as a tempest, strikingly furious and benignly short. There were not even the strains of a dirge; one could only sense the stillness of a graveyard. For a moment, every one of the author's siblings probably wondered they had lost a brother. The author knew almost surely that Pa had disowned him at least at that point in time; he could do nothing else but to pull himself together. The only hopeful one was Mie, his mother. She beckoned everyone to return to his or her tasks without a sound. Similarly, she pulled the author aside to offer wise counsel for him to speak no more for that evening. Mie was literally the calm in the storm. There was a death in the house, death of the author; he, however, felt as though he was the only one alive. Every mind in the house quickened to wonder what would happen in the days to follow, a solemn mood rested on each to imagine the worst. For the author the worst had passed. His work laid out providentially for him: to tell and share the gospel to Pa, to Mie, and to every sibling of his. It must surely begin with Pa; his upbringing had taught him this was a truthful and righteous thing to not subvert the authority of the head of the family. He could not proselytise within the family against Pa's silent will and iron hand. He resolved to live his Christian life faithfully and perchance the Lord shall convict those hearts at home to come on the Christian ship. Yet it must wait and for a long while; some pains deep as they were, do not heal or fade quickly. *He that loveth father or mother more than me is not worthy of me: and he that loveth son or daughter more than me is not worthy of me.*—Matthew 10:37

Pa had drawn the line in the sand, and in a sense, the author was now free to begin his work in completely following Christ. In looking back, it was as though the Lord chose the time for this all to happen, a time he was a man, an adult, independent from the holds of family and kinship, a time when the objections saw little room to viably cull up a storm. It was at a time when Buddhism had died in him, also jaded in Pa; the brunt of shock and of pain was easier to bear altogether. *If any man come to me, and hate not his father, and mother, and wife, and children, and brethren, and sisters, yea, and his own life also, he cannot be my disciple.*—Luke 14:26. This verse, when first read may appear as shocking. In having been through this situation, he can truly attest how the Lord knew it all. Christ did not demand us to hate our parents and kin, but He must truly have first place in our priorities, above parents and kin. There is no room for compromise when we follow Christ; it must be complete surrender. Let the dead, those who refuses Christ, bury their dead: both the physically and the spiritually dead. *Jesus said unto him, Let the dead bury their dead: but go thou and preach the kingdom of God.* Luke 9:60. *And Jesus said unto him, No man, having put his hand to the plough, and looking back, is fit for the kingdom of God.*—Luke 9:62.

His Love will not spare. Continuing in the above Scriptural account, Jesus looked on the young man and loved him! But He read him through and through and mercifully gave the unwelcome verdict: *Yet lackest thou one thing: sell all that thou hast, and distribute unto the poor, and thou shalt have treasure in heaven: and come, follow me.*—Luke 18:22. The young man went away sad, and Christ went away sad! But He loves us too well to spare us! God's love is consistent with stern dealings at those things that may cause us to fail of the best. When we have decided to follow Christ, we must act decisively to go forth in faith setting aside any hesitation from discouragement, from fear of reprisal, from self-pride, and from possible loss. This may seem humanly inconceivable and yet faithfully possible in His love and providence.

We believe in God's love when all evidences seem not so. "We have known," says the Apostle, that "God is love," unutterable and changeless! But there are times when we have to believe in it, when shrouded in the perplexity over life's problems. We often face incidents and providences that strike us as inconsistent with God's Love. Then we must believe that the same love is there. God Is Love, and nothing can reach us save through His Love.

When disowned by our own, when disavowed by the world, we can take comfort that God owns us; Christ adopted us into His joy, into His Kingdom, into everlasting life. As adopted sons of God, we have access to God and can lay hold on all benefits and privileges of son-ship in the name of Jesus Christ. Verily, we are in the best station in life.

# 3

## Christianity a Vocation, not a Profession

*Whereby are given unto us great and precious promises: that by*
*these ye might be partakers of the Divine Nature.*
—2 Peter 1:4.

I am now a Christian, a follower of the Christ, Jesus Christ. That is
the full name of my Master and Saviour. What does it mean? I had
absolutely no clue whatsoever. God was clearly my sure portion, Jesus
Christ my closest confidant, the Holy Spirit my counsel and comforter,
this earth my temporal lodge, and heaven my eternal home. Today, I know
'Christ' means 'Anointed', the Greek translation of the Hebrew word
rendered 'Messiah', the official title of our Lord, occurring five hundred
and fourteen times in the New Testament. It defines Him as one anointed
for or consecrated to his great redemptive work as saviour of his people.
He is Jesus (His earthly Hebrew name) the Christ, the Anointed One.

We are called not to be professors. We can only profess Christ when we
know Him in actuality. Those who do not know Him cannot profess Him;
there is no truth at the back of their profession. Such professors are not
saved if they do not follow the way, seek the truth, and live the life. They
certainly will be cast into hell. *If a man abide not in me, he is cast forth as*

*a branch, and is withered; and men gather them, and cast them into the fire, and they are burned.*—John 15:6

What makes a Christian? We can only simply suppose a follower of Christ, to obey His command to preach to the world that the church of Christ may be established in His good pleasure. *And when he had found him, he brought him unto Antioch. And it came to pass, that a whole year they assembled themselves with the church, and taught much people. And the disciples were called Christians first in Antioch*—Acts11:26.

*Profession* is an open declaration; public avowal or acknowledgment of one's sentiments or beliefs; as professions of friendship or sincerity; a profession of faith or religion. *Vocation* is a calling by the will of God; or the bestowment of God's distinguishing grace upon a person, which puts that person in the way of salvation. *Profession is man's declaration; vocation is God's calling.* In the former, man can declare but may never act according to the declaration. In the latter, God calls and man must act according to that call. Man impelled by God's call, and so impelled by God's grace, is compelled to follow Christ.

A follower connotes one who comes, goes, or moves after Christ, in the same course. It is one that takes Christ as his guide in doctrines, opinions, or example; one who receives the opinions, and imitates the example of Christ; an adherent; an imitator of Christ. Assuredly, we are followers of Christ. We completely believe all that Scripture reveals of Jesus, the Son of God who died for all that we may not hopelessly die in sin, but rose with Christ a new creature to everlasting life.

A Christian certainly is not a mere believer but also one who lives out his beliefs and convictions as he imitates Christ. He is a practitioner not a mere professor. The Christian is a *real* believer who 'walks and talks' of Christ, who lives and breathes Christ; not a *nominal* believer known only in name yet lives otherwise in his old practices of waywardness. The real believer knows the deep abyss of sin that he is in and repents, turns from it, turns to God for succour, and looks up to Christ, to the cross for salvation. *And he that taketh not his cross, and followeth after me, is not worthy of me.*—Matthew 10:38

The Christian did not come into the fellowship of other believers to embrace some high-minded intellectual thought, idea, or philosophy reserved for a class of brilliant, highly intelligent, or aristocratic people specially endowed with some such innate characteristics uncommon to the general populace. He did not join an intellectual society of earthly luminaries to argue or debate an idea or philosophy, to speculate on what is or why it is. The believer centres his all in Christ, the fountain of life everlasting, of enduring truth, and infinite wisdom.

What does it mean to be a Christian? We cannot be only a mere professor of all that Jesus the Christ is, of His Person in the triune God (the Father, the Son, and the Holy Spirit), of His role in our salvation, of His life, and all that He taught and did. The profession transforms our way of thinking, and translates us into activists for the Lord, compelled by His love and mercy. We must bear witness of His intrinsic value. He had transformed us and we are no longer conformed to the world, in its workings, and in its assessments of value. Yet all this transformation was possible not out of our own 'goodness'—for truly we have none—but verily by the counsel of the Holy Spirit that God gave us that we may not be comfortless. *Opening and alleging, that Christ must needs have suffered, and risen again from the dead; and that this Jesus, whom I preach unto you, is Christ*—Acts 17:3. *And when Silas and Timotheus were come from Macedonia, Paul was pressed in the spirit, and testified to the Jews that Jesus was Christ*—Acts 18:5.

The prophet Isaiah spoke of Christ as saviour: *The Spirit of the Lord GOD is upon me; because the LORD hath anointed me to preach good tidings unto the meek; he hath sent me to bind up the brokenhearted, to proclaim liberty to the captives, and the opening of the prison to them that are bound*—Isaiah 61:1. *The Spirit of the Lord GOD is upon me; because the LORD hath anointed me to preach good tidings unto the meek; he hath sent me to bind up the brokenhearted, to proclaim liberty to the captives, and the opening of the prison to them that are bound*—Daniel 9:24. Thus spoke Daniel who wrote of him as "Messiah the Prince" (Daniel 9:25). He came for the sake of the Jews with whom God had a covenant. *But he answered and said, I am not sent but unto the lost sheep of the house of Israel*—Matthew 15:24.

Christ, lifted up on the cross, died, and rose on the third day, His redemptive work accomplished for *all* who believe that His shed blood took away all our sins. We are children of Adam's *disobedience*, clearly and undeniably, the evidence of sin. We partook of that sinful nature in and of ourselves, and perpetuated sin. Christ gave of Himself in *obedience* to God the Father to once and for all put sin to death so as to raise us in triumph in the new life in Him. *And as Moses lifted up the serpent in the wilderness, even so must the Son of man be lifted up: that whosoever believeth in him should not perish, but have eternal life*—John 3:14-15. *And I, if I be lifted up from the earth, will draw all men unto me*—John 12:32. We must look up to Christ, to the cross where He wrought His redemptive work for our salvation, not to look at, or about the world. Christ came for Israel's sake, and for the world; to all who believe in Him, they shall have everlasting life.

This was a great benefit, a gifted privilege from the Highest, indeed a greatly valuable treasure. Christ came as man to accomplish His redemptive work for His people by dying on the cross. He was the Anointed of God, the Messiah, prophesied to be King of the Jews. How was His dying on the cross a benefit of great value? It would seem at first pass, a death of a pauper; for crucifixion was an instrument of miserable, and painful death intended for a slave. The Jews detest the cross as an instrument of death. *Christ hath redeemed us from the curse of the law, being made a curse for us: for it is written, Cursed is every one that hangeth on a tree.*—Galatians 3:13.

How can we coherently hold together that Divine law of God's righteousness—He hates sin and would never restrain or withhold His righteous wrath—the unchanging law that binds the universe, yet how was it possible for God to welcome and receive the law breaker? How can heaven reveal the hate of God for sin, and yet show His love for every sinner?

God, in His infinite wisdom, in His righteousness and mercy resolved for us in time preternal, and which solved for us, the infinite marvel of the cross of Christ. When we have understood the purpose of the cross of Christ, we can never doubt the *righteousness of God*. When we have understood the cross of Christ, we never can doubt the *love of God* again. And so in my experience, I have come to understand in the very depths of my being that God hates sin with a consuming hatred, and at the same time that He loves me with an unquestionable, unwavering, unflagging, and unconditional love of a divine Father. *Righteousness without mercy* cannot save me, for I have broken every commandment, every moral law of God. Righteousness is God's unchanging nature: grace and mercy is God's answer to man's hopelessness. Still, *mercy without justice* cannot save me, for the impress of the moral law is set on my heart. When I come to the feet of the Lord Jesus Christ, and let His love fill my soul, then righteousness and love are reconciled. Christ's death on the cross and His shed blood covers me and you to *justify* us (make right and just) before a righteous God, for Christ lived a sinless life as man and died in obedience to His Father's will. He stood before God as truly the only worthy sacrifice to redeem us. He became ransom as the Son of man by His death on the cross, as the price of ransom to satisfy God's demand for justice for our sins, to satisfy the holiness and justice of God's character and His fundamental moral law. We are debtors to God's law, and Christ was ransom in payment of the debt we owed to Divine justice.

Knowing Jesus as a person in the Bible, His Deity; knowing Him as my Lord and the only One who was able to reconcile my broken relationship with and separation from God. Knowing His nature and His character was the foundation and the critical cornerstone of my Christian faith. Everywhere I turned, in every situation encountered, He was the *answer* in every human interaction with which I came face to face: Jesus was ever present to reveal man's waywardness and God's righteousness.

In my constant commune with Him in intimate fellowship in daily walk, I became consciously aware of His workings and presence. Only in having first learned to know Him intimately in the private spheres of life, where His heart touches our heart, and the delicate contentions of conscience are not over laden by the present difficulties in the natural world or the intricate shifts of the world's religious, social, economic, and political order. It would take many purposeful hammerings of the hot and fiery iron on the anvil of sturdy faith to set us in tandem with providential time and circumstance. Afterwards, He guides our entry to the larger arenas of the Christian religion, without risk of losing our faith, our sensibility, or our conscience. God approves us by His testing in His loving way, that we may truly see Christ. It is to Him that we turn, who is the very foundation and chief cornerstone of our faith. Once the foundation is set, the living cornerstone directs the position of all the *lively stones in the building of the spiritual house.* (1 Peter 2:4-9). The plumb line, a measure of perpendicular straightness of a wall, by Him is set; from Him all standards are drawn. His Divine standard cannot move to suit man's whims and fancies. He judges every deviation—minute or glaring—from it. *Thus he shewed me: and, behold, the Lord stood upon a wall made by a plumbline, with a plumbline in his hand. And the LORD said unto me, Amos, what seest thou? And I said, a plumbline. Then said the Lord, Behold, I will set a plumbline in the midst of my people Israel: I will not again pass by them any more.*—Amos 7:7-8. In Him is our anchor, we remain unflinchingly grounded, unperturbed, and untroubled in the face of raging and consuming storms. *Which hope we have as an anchor of the soul, both sure and stedfast, and which entereth into that within the veil.*—Hebrews 6:19.

This did not happen in an instant or in a short space of months or a year or two. It would take a lifetime as I have now learnt. And so we are urged to walk, if not, trudge onward and upward, ever trusting in Jesus to lead the way, *His Word as a lamp unto our feet and a light unto our path.* (Psalm 119:105). Moreover, our faith is a vocation attested by the fact that Christ is ever with us, in our midst, to make that calling sure.

*Christ is ever in the midst of His brethren. That is His inheritance, so that we can have a precious inheritance indeed.* He is among us, yet heir of the Kingdom of Heaven. We, adopted in Christ, and made co-heirs with Him; He sealed the rights of our adoption eternally. While here on earth as man, *And Jesus saith unto him, The foxes have holes, and the birds of the air have nests; but the Son of man hath not where to lay his head*—Matthew 8:20. We can take great comfort that He is our brethren ever in our midst in heaven and in earth.

*Christ was there in the midst on the Cross.* On the cross, Christ in His humility and obedience to God the Father, was for the world a curse, a shame. Yet on the cross, Christ revealed His eminence as the only worthy saviour for man, *where they crucified him, and two other with him, on either side one, and Jesus in the midst.*—John 19:18

*He was numbered with the transgressors* (Mark 15:28). Forasmuch as we partook of flesh and blood, He shared the same; and since we were under the curse of a broken law, He also bowed beneath its weight, and made a curse for us. Christ took the mid-current of pain; where the force was most severe, the burden overbearing. There the Lamb of God bore the sin of the world. God appointed on Him to meet the iniquities of us all. Equally, in the same manner of those who refuse, as did the one thief (*if thou be Christ, save thyself and us*), and of those who accept (*remember me when thou comest into thy kingdom*), as did the other.

*Christ is in the midst, in the gathering of His People.* "Where two or three are gathered together in my name, there am I in the midst of them." (Matthew 18:20). He is the centre of unity for His own. We come from different quarters with our peculiar prepossessions, predispositions, and preconceptions, with no special affinity to each other; but in touching Him, we become one with all who touch Him also. Let us be watchful that we give our devoted attention to Christ always and in all things. Let Him be the centre of our home life, our social, and business life under all circumstances.

*Christ is in the midst in Heaven.* "For the Lamb which is in the midst of the throne shall feed them, and shall lead them unto living fountains of waters: and God shall wipe away all tears from their eyes." (Revelation 7:17). All beings in heaven and in earth revolve around Jesus as their common centre. Jesus is the heart of heaven, the sun of paradise, the essence of its bliss, the centre of its love, the innermost Soul of its life. Christ is the Life of our innermost soul.

Our Christian faith is a gift of God. It is precious above all else. Let us recognise with no hesitation that our God's grace answers man's every sin, misery, and helplessness. Let us honour God with our lives in our Christian vocation and not merely in profession.

### Notes

Christianity is uniquely about following Christ, not a set of beliefs, doctrines, ideas, thoughts, or practices. Christ is at the centre of Christianity. All that Christians do in their lives reflect on Christ's person and characteristically of His nature. Christ dwells in them; it cannot be a mere profession. Adopted in Christ; they live in the power of God imparted to us by the Holy Spirit. *As for me, I will behold thy face in righteousness: I shall be satisfied, when I awake, with thy likeness.*—Psalm 17:15.

We are as branches of the Lord, we draw from Him; He is the vine, we are the branches. *I am the true vine, and my Father is the husbandman.*—John 15:1. *I am the vine, ye are the branches: He that abideth in me, and I in him, the same bringeth forth much fruit: for without me ye can do nothing.*—John 15:5. We are as trees of the Lord, the cedars of Lebanon. We are fruitful when we are in Him, drawing from His grace, from His beauty. *The trees of the LORD are full of sap; the cedars of Lebanon, which he hath planted; where the birds make their nests: as for the stork, the fir trees are her house*— Psalm 104:16-17.

We are the sons of God. We shall only walk as sons of God. We shall not walk as sons of perdition. The sons of God have no alliance with the sons of perdition. We walk by faith in the Life of Christ, in obedience to God, in His light. We do not walk in disobedience to, in murmuring of, and in conflict with God; we do not walk in darkness. *Beloved, now are we the sons of God, and it doth not yet appear what we shall be: but we know that, when he shall appear, we shall be like him; for we shall see him as he is*—1 John 3:2.

Sin and punishment closely knitted as pleasure to 'riot' and the 'reward' of unrighteousness drawn in a correlation, sets man at odds with the righteousness and faith that God favours. Sin defiles as spots and blemishes. Brethren, let us keep our Christian vocation pure and undefiled for God's glory. *And shall receive the reward of unrighteousness, as they that count it pleasure to riot in the day time. Spots they are and blemishes, sporting themselves with their own deceivings while they feast with you.*—2 Peter 2:13

Shall we reap where we have not sown? Labour for things above, labour of our souls for heaven is a blessing; labour of our bodies for the benefits of this world is a curse. Be earnest in effort; be prompt in endeavour, to study, and to labour so as to make our divine calling sure. *Wherefore the rather, brethren, give diligence to make your calling and election sure: for if ye do these things, ye shall never fall: for so an entrance shall be ministered unto you abundantly into the everlasting kingdom of our Lord and Saviour Jesus Christ.*—2 Peter 1:10-11

# 4

## JOIN a Church.
## WHAT is a church?
## WHICH church?

*And when he had found him, he brought him unto Antioch.*
*And it came to pass, that a whole year they assembled themselves*
*with the church, and taught much people. And the disciples were*
*called Christians first in Antioch.*
—Acts 11:26

The first thought after becoming a Christian was to join a church. Newly born in Christ and indwelt with the Holy Spirit, the promptings therefrom cause one to seek out other Christians, saints in the church of Christ. Yet, in all of the limitations that a young Christian mind possesses, I could only think of the physical tangible church populated by Christians—real or nominal—whose object was to gather together to perform corporate Christian duties.

What is a church? The Bible describes the church as a garden or vineyard, in which the Divine Spirit is ever at work, tending, directing, inspiring, and calling to co-operate with Him all His servants, whether they be Paul, Apollos, or Cephas. God's Word is the blueprint. In *pre*-Christian history, the church was a theocratic society, community or 'congregation' of God's chosen people, the Jews. In Christian history, the church was a theocratic democracy where it was a society of those who are free but are always conscious that their freedom springs from obedience to their God. A systematic doctrine of the church was never anywhere in Christian history, yet there were features and characteristics that existed. The church has *faith* in its 'building' and perseverance as declared by Christ Himself: *upon this rock I will build my church; and the gates of hell shall not prevail against it* (Matthew 16:18). There must be *fellowship* among members within the church, each Christian directly joined to Christ, and therefore are members one of another. *So we, being many, are one body in Christ, and every one members one of another*—Romans 12:5.

The church is as a vast 'building', raised through the ages, requiring labourers to lay the foundations, others to build the walls, and others yet, to put the final touches in the light of an accomplished purpose. In each case, the design, the successive stages of advancing progress, the engagement of the workers, the direction of their labours and their reward is entirely with God who is the Husbandman and the Master-builder. It is not our work, but His; we are not responsible for the results, but only to do His will; He repays us by generous rewards, but there our responsibility ends. When the garden stands in the mature beauty, and yields the prolific fruit as intended; when the building is completed and stands in symmetrical glory, then those who have co-operated will stand aside, and *God may be all in all* (1 Corinthians 15:28). *The husbandman that laboureth must be first partaker of the fruits*—1 Timothy 2:6. *Be patient therefore, brethren, unto the coming of the Lord. Behold, the husbandman waiteth for the precious fruit of the earth, and hath long patience for it, until he receive the early and latter rain*—James 5:7.

In the church, the same law prevails in man's co-operation with God. God has given the Word, but preachers need to proclaim it. The words of inspiration burn with the fire of God, but man translates them into every language under heaven. Man must read and study the Word that illuminates with what God will reveal to him. The saving power of Christ waits to heal and bless, but He needs the co-operation of the human hand and life as the medium through which His virtue passes. Those whom God calls into fellowship in serving others can count on Him for the supply of all their needs. *Therefore let no man glory in men. For all things are yours;*

*whether Paul, or Apollos, or Cephas, or the world, or life, or death, or things present, or things to come; all are yours; and ye are Christ's; and Christ is God's.*—1 Co 3:21-23.

What do I look for in a church? Back then, I was clueless about what to look for in a church. The best logical thing to do was go to one and try it out awhile. If I think, in all my limitations, that the church taught the things I have read in the gospels, then I stayed a little longer to go through the 'works' (Bible study, church attendance, soul winning, activities, etc.) to better understand if that was the church described in the Bible. The church must be Bible-believing, no extra-Biblical beliefs and practices; all things must be tested in the Word. I knew nothing beyond the four gospels for a start. There was far much to do to be able to organise one's thoughts coherently and discern the truth. Overall, my experience at church-going had been generally chaotic and seemingly long to arrive at a sure understanding of what it should be. Still, in all things God lets us serve out time according to His divine plan, not a moment too soon, not a moment late. Even well-meaning Christians can end up in the wrong church for many reasons such as preconceived notions or lack of them, non-Christian 'tolerance' (a dangerous idea), image projected by the church, the comfortable setting, music, methods, practices, people, Bible version used, and so on. The danger that lurked about was comfort, where one can stay too long to want a move even though aware of questionable doctrine and practices. How can we have that kind of conviction as a young Christian? Yet, the key reason is our lack of a Biblical understanding of a church; that, we can attribute to a young faith not adequately familiar with Scripture nor an exposure to discussion of the subject. The more matured Christian has no excuse for not knowing though. The church must therefore attend to the maturing of a young Christian's foundational Scriptural knowledge and understanding. That would certainly lend him to an enduring witness for Christ. As long as our desire for God is deep and long, we can be sure of His watchful care and providence to remove us from the valleys of the shadows and into the clear and exhilarating mountaintops of abundant and eternal mercies.

What do I now do? With the priceless treasure that God gifted me, I must now apply watchful stewardship over it. My responsibility is immense. There was no checklist that told me what I needed to do as a Christian.

One had to figure it out by faith and diligence. What made that possible? Our affections for Christ, for the truth He spoke about, His tug on our hearts, on our conscience, make us up to be Christians. A regenerate man, born again into the light, into the knowledge of the truth, into the knowledge of God, under His authority, under His grace and mercy—that was the Christian. There was no rule book, no checklist, no list that moves the will of man to align with God's will. It is God's light sent to man as the Comforter when our Lord Jesus ascended to heaven to continue His work on the right hand of God, forever interceding for man. In that, the Father gave us the Holy Spirit who dwells in us, convicting us, pricking our conscience, prompting us to function as He directs. The Holy Spirit of God works for God by us that we may glorify Him in all we do. God did not leave us comfortless. God gave us His inspired Word to reveal of Himself, to illumine our hearts and minds in all that the Word will teach us. *In the beginning was the Word, and the Word was with God, and the Word was God.*—John 1:1-2. *And the Word was made flesh, and dwelt among us (and we beheld his glory, the glory as of the only begotten of the Father,) full of grace and truth.*—John 1:14

What's next? I must tell the world of this great treasure of immense value. I must share with all others so that they can partake in the gifted privilege and enjoy its attendant benefits.

## Notes

The notes below under different headers were unknown to my young Christian mind in the early days of my conversion. It was as walking into walls, adjusting to hit another, and still others, until one finds a clear way. It would do well for new Christians to consider them when choosing a church to begin their Christian journey. There is not a perfect church; the church is still in the process of perfecting for the Second Coming of Christ. The important thing to watch for and to note is that the church's teachings and practices must prove Scriptural. We have the Word of God for reference and for guidance.

**The Lord's Day** is the first day of the week, which is Sunday. The appearance of Sunday as the one distinctive day for worship was almost certainly evident from the days of the early church. Sunday, however, was sharply distinguished from the Sabbath. The former was the day on which worship was offered in a specifically Christian (in the New Testament church) form, the other was a day of ritual rest to be observed by all who were subject to the Law of Moses through circumcision (Galatians 5:3; compare Acts 21:20). Uncircumcised Gentiles, however, were free from any obligation of Sabbath observance. The Sabbath rest was a memorial of the creation of the world, still one day—the seventh day—out of seven. The Sabbath was retained in apostolic times as a memorial to the new creation when Christ was resurrected on the first day of the week; hence a commemoration of the creation of the world as well as the more superior work of redemption. Scripturally, in apostolic times there was no renewal of any Sabbath rules or transfer of them to Sunday, the first day of the week, for Gentile converts. General apostolic practice fixed Sunday as the day for public Christian worship. The Lord's Day on the first day of the week became the Christian Sabbath. *And upon the first day of the week, when the disciples came together to break bread, Paul preached unto them, ready to depart on the morrow; and continued his speech until midnight—* Acts 20:7. *Upon the first day of the week let every one of you lay by him in store, as God hath prospered him, that there be no gatherings when I come.—*1 Corinthians 16:2.

**Church membership:** It is the difference in character and gifts of individual Christians that leads Paul to speak of the variety of members, which, though of manifold functions, are equally important to the completeness of the body. It is thus in the manifold variety of the body of Christ (1 Corinthians 12:12-27; Ephesians 4:16), and Christians being members of Christ, who is the head (Ephesians 1:22; 4:15; 5:23), are members one of another (Romans 12:5; Ephesians 4:25). Membership requires a commitment to the church, to its 'building' plan, and to its maturing until the Lord comes; a commitment to fellowship with its members, in building each other for God's glory. Membership to a church usually begins with baptism, one of two church ordinances instituted by the Lord, after which the member enters into other areas of service in ministry to the church as the Lord calls. *In whom all the building fitly framed together groweth unto an holy temple in the Lord.—*Ephesians 2:21

**Ordinances**: Baptism and The Lord's Supper are the two ordinances instituted by Christ, commanded by Him. Ordinances imply an established practice generally fixed in nature.

Baptism as an ordinance had been a cause of much division among churches through the ages. The significance of baptism is in its *representation* of the death of Christ on the cross. By the ordinance of baptism, we are buried with Him (into death), and raised with Him (from the dead). It is performed in the presence of the church whereby the baptised acknowledges his understanding and willingness to follow the Lord. When he tells outsiders he is baptised, he shows himself a Christian and witnesses to the world thus. *What shall we say then? Shall we continue in sin, that grace may abound? God forbid. How shall we, that are dead to sin, live any longer therein? Know ye not, that so many of us as were baptized into Jesus Christ were baptized into his death? Therefore we are buried with him by baptism into death: that like as Christ was raised up from the dead by the glory of the Father, even so we also should walk in newness of life. For if we have been planted together in the likeness of his death, we shall be also in the likeness of his resurrection:*—Romans 6:1-5

In the case of The Lord's Supper, *"Do this in remembrance of me,"* (1 Corinthians 11:24-25) with reference to both the bread and the cup reminds communicants of Christ. How necessary is the performance of this ordinance in reminding us of Christ and of His redemptive work for us, in strengthening our faith as believers and as a witness to the world of the life in Christ. Paul adds, *"As oft as ye eat this bread and drink this cup, ye do show forth the Lord's death until He comes"* (1 Corinthians 11:26) is a testimony to outsiders of the fact of His death on the cross, that will be perpetuated until His coming. And He is coming anytime soon.

**Statement of Faith (SOF):** Faith implies a creed as a confession and testimony, as it answers to a natural impulse of the soul. Hence, a profession of faith is at once a personal, a social and a historical testimony. A formal creed witnesses to the universality of faith, binds believers together, and unites the successive ages of the church. It is the spontaneous expression of the life and experience of the Christian society. The systematic statement of religious faith is the formal expression of 'the faith which was delivered unto the saints'. The SOF draws from Scriptural foundation and rudimentary

Biblical statements upon which the distinctive dogmas the church based its faith.

On the whole, the SOF is a comprehensive summary of truth, laying down the rule of faith as a foundation, following out its issues of good or evil. True belief must cohere closely with right action. The institutional churches generally applied a common creed and a similar SOF, while independent churches crafted their own. By institutional churches, I mean the Roman Catholics church, and those that branched from it during and since the Reformation.

# 5

## Win Souls by Preaching the GOSPEL

*And the lord said unto the servant, Go out into the highways and hedges, and compel them to come in, that my house may be filled. For I say unto you, That none of those men which were bidden shall taste of my supper.*
—Luke 14:23-24.

*For though I preach the gospel, I have nothing to glory of: for necessity is laid upon me; yea, woe is unto me, if I preach not the gospel! For if I do this thing willingly, I have a reward: but if against my will, a dispensation of the gospel is committed unto me.*
—1 Corinthians 9:16-17.

In 1994, *The New York Times* reported that graffiti from the 1800s was discovered by workers renovating the Washington Monument. It was quite a different tone from much of the graffiti found today on walls, railcars, and street signs. Here's what it said:

*Whoever is the human instrument under God in the conversion of one soul, erects a monument to his own memory more lofty and enduring than this.*

The inscription had for its signatory, the initials *BFB*. No one knew who that was, but this anonymous author's words spoke of soul winning.

Faith in Christ was a very personal experience. Still very early in the faith, my inability to frame my conversion without any 'fireworks' was simply incredulous for anyone to apprehend. I was not as a bad boy suddenly turned good boy, on a hundred and eighty degree turnaround, catching everyone's notice. My conversion was not dramatic or 'magical'. Most people thought of me as a 'good boy', how much better could I get? Or if someone thought I was a bad boy, how bad could I get? How can anyone understand my experience that was really very straightforward in nature? There was no discernible immediate instantaneous outward manifestation that anyone could see as being different from the 'old creature'. All that I could explain was that I saw in Christ, God Himself; that drew me near to Him as drawn through the veil. His love and mercy was unmistakable. I felt at liberty to live in His will, in His way, and in His truth. Alas, it was not about who I was, how good or bad I was. If it was, then all things are simply *relative*. I am truly grateful it was all about Christ, who is better than good or bad; He is perfect. He is God; there is no variation about Him. He is *absolute*. He is sure.

Should I tell anyone at all? Do I quietly go about my business as though nothing had happened that I ruffled or offended no one, and that no one offended me? These were questions that first came to mind after my conversion. Being a Christian was a great experience and I was not able to simply bottle it. Its fragrance I had to share; its seal broken, the bottle I had to uncork. I was proud to be Christian, I told everyone I met, wrote it in the forms that had a request for religion to be stated, in my resume, and in anything that required me to declare my religion. I was bubbling with joy in the new life, full of energy, overflowing with enthusiasm; it was a highly precious gift of God. I was not embarrassed to be a follower of Christ, how could I be for I adored Jesus for all that he was to me then. I was proud of Him, my saviour, my elder brother, my leader, my example.

How do I share with Pa and Mie? There were several hurdles to overcome. Their unflinching *objection* was the biggest one, but in a stormy exchange, irreversible and firm showdown with Pa; that surprisingly settled as a summer tempest, frightfully quick tempered and brief. I was without fear when I broke the news to Pa; a boldness that was beyond my own comprehension. *Language* was the next biggest one. With Pa and Mie, my grasp of the Fujian dialect was very basic, too basic to express any Christian truths. English was a language at which Pa and Mie were completely limited. Does sharing the Word of Life with them lie here dead in the dust? *Assuredly, the answer is 'No'. I had prayed that the Lord must cause their conversion to happen; it did not happen anytime soon and took nearly two decades before it came to pass. It did not happen through my witness, as they would not listen to a renegade son. However, by God's grace, it came about through a circuitous route of people and happenings. All in all, the Lord was truly gracious and merciful to them. The Lord was faithful to my importunate and unceasing petitions in prayer and supplication. Pa and Mie ultimately became Christians and have now passed into glory. I praise the Lord for His grace and for His faithfulness.* Language seemingly an obstacle to telling others, was not really so: for the Lord shall guide all things unto Himself in accordance with His will, calling whom He has foreordained, and predestinated since the foundations of the world; He will cause them to be holy and duly removed to glory in His kingdom.

How do I tell my siblings? This was less difficult as all my siblings had the facility of the English language. My brother Cai, a year younger, and closest to me, came to know the Lord a year after my conversion. He tagged along with me to church on Sundays some months after the dust settled at home. My youngest sister converted through a lady friend of mine at the Youth for Christ and 3:16 Music Ministry. This friend happened to teach my sister at a secondary school. Another younger brother was a member of the Boys' Brigade at school where they had a Christian ministry and he was duly converted. My eldest sister married, moved out, and eventually migrated to Holland; she is still unconverted. Only one other sister in Singapore remains unconverted as at the time of writing. Can you see the hand of God in all of these conversions in my family? They did not happen in the straight line fashion my natural common mind envisaged; they came about in God's own way and in His own time. We simply do not have the wherewithal to hasten and force it.

How did I tell my relatives? That was relatively easy. When uncles and aunts asked Pa or Mie where I was, they would respond with a simple short "in church" that appeared as the only answer that distinctly reveal

I had become a Christian. That saved me much explanation when I meet them sometime later. My parents had broken the news for me. Relatives could never understand the deep embarrassment Pa and Mie bore in their bosoms, for these relatives were either agnostics or believers in Taoism or ancestral worship. They believed in religious tolerance.

How do I tell my friends, and the world? Those Christian friends from school and National Service with whom I was still in touch, I shared with them my conversion that they may rejoice with me. Other non-Christian friends came to know of it by circumstance. How they thought, I never speculated nor was it important or necessary. My Buddhist ties had ended at my conversion, and everything else with any semblance of a link, came to a complete halt. Pa would have felt deeply embarrassed and greatly irked if I ever stepped foot in the temple.

Thought precedes action. Soul winning requires of us constancy in thought for lost souls, a heart that grieves for their lack of knowledge of our Lord Jesus Christ, and a life zealous for reaching lost souls to draw them into the light, to have them sit at the foot of Jesus to listen to His gospel. We must be as Paul doing his uttermost in reaching out to the unsaved, whether we can or cannot even bring a soul to Christ. *To the weak became I as weak, that I might gain the weak: I am made all things to all men, that I might by all means save some.*—1 Corinthians 9:22. We must lay aside every weight and forge forward that we may win an incorruptible crown for the praise and honour of our Lord.

## Notes

**Youth for Christ (YFC)** was a Christian youth movement that reached out to schools. With its headquarters based at the Bible House in Armenian Street, it planted youth leaders in schools and had quite a substantial following. I met its president while at a Reservists in-camp training. After the in-camp stint was completed, I visited the YFC headquarters, and happily learnt they had a small music ministry with a combo band along with a growing group of singers and choreographers. They would take a trumpeter and so I joined as it was for the Lord. We performed in Singapore and went to evangelise to youths in Thailand at a juvenile reformatory, in schools, and churches. It was essentially evangelism through music and choreography. I gave a testimony of my conversion to a whole school of teenagers. At the end of it, when we mingled with the students did I realise the adverse significant gap in their grasp of English. Did they not understand all that I shared of my conversion and the gospel message? Did I share it in vain? Was it without purpose? It was on this evangelism outing that the Thais gave me my Christian name 'Robin' as in Robin Hood. I came away blessed with all that the experience had to offer, yet deep in my soul, I felt miserably wretched as a failure. There was no way of doing things differently as I was under authority of the group I was a member. Again, service and ministry were on my mind, never how we delivered them. I could only come away knowing I had the best of intentions just as my other fellow workers had, yet it was as thoroughly frustrating in that we had put the cart before the horse. The work was done but without the results or the fruits thereof. I learnt that in all things, we must offer our efforts as sacrifice before the Lord for Him to direct them in His Spirit. We cannot think, 'engineer', and 'drive' our own efforts in His work. He is ever the Driver.

**3:16 Music Ministry** was a breakaway from the YFC and became independent from YFC support. The music ministry at YFC essentially became defunct as its members moved en bloc to 3:16. The author channelled a substantial portion of his monthly income to the support of an independent 3:16 ministry, just as did a few of the other members who were in gainful employment. A majority of the members were still at school, placing the financial burden squarely on the shoulders of the working dozen or so. As an evangelising music group, its effectiveness in winning souls to Christ clearly limited by a lack of maturity of leaders and followers, as well as the unwieldy young peoples' relationship issues inherent in such groups. Christian maturity was in want and the endeavour would fade in effectiveness.

**Billy Graham Crusade** (BGC) was the author's first and only exposure to mega evangelising outreach on a national scale. Months before the event, the local daily newspapers regularly ran a full page of a teasing single catchy worded questions such as "Do you know?" or "What is it?" with no additional information provided. That created much discussion over the suspense and taunting anticipation of that which would come to pass. Churches of different denominations supported the crusade effort by sending their members to receive organised training by BGC. The author went to several of the training sessions and received packaged materials to prepare him for outreach before and after the Crusade. A little palm-sized booklet containing a simple 3 or 4-pointer message of salvation with a short prayer became the basis for reaching out to unbelievers as firstly a hand out followed by praying with them to accept Christ. In today's context, we call this 'quick prayerism' where the salvation message is often considered over simplified and glossed over with an assumed appreciation. The message of Christ dying for the world, and for all sinners, taken at face value meant that the soul seeking salvation had little understanding of why that must be. The understanding lacking, there was no compelling call to the place of certain repentance. No conjecture intended, but it was as though the suppliant in his prayer for salvation was seeking comfort that he had performed his part in satisfaction for a secured life in eternity. Oh, can one solicit salvation by mere words?

The author went through heart wrenching moments when he went out to the heartlands where young and old truly were lost. His inability to handle dialects proficiently when attempting to share the gospel with middle aged and older folks, etched in his experience the complete inadequacy of man in the outreach and conversion process. How does one take the loving message of God, from God's Word, to man under sin and in darkness from the truth? How is man 'called'? Do we reach out to those not called? Called or not, only God knew. We should not ask that question. Is outreach futile? It cannot be so, for Christ commanded us to preach to the world. We shall go forth in faith in Christ, in the knowledge of our desire and also of our ability or lack of it. We need to hone our abilities for the Lord's work, and be diligent in acquiring knowledge of the truth to effectively share the good news. We must commit ourselves to prayer and devotion for lost souls.

At the completion of the week of rallies and outreach, volunteers returned to their church of sending and went about life as usual. The evangelising fervour generated through BGC was highly infectious and had a strong imprint on the author's soul winning experience then and in a long time afterwards. The method, he felt was inadequate—as he had experienced—questioningly short in giving the receiver of the gospel the exact message Christ would have intended. The goal appeared to focus on getting to 'yes' to all the questions, and the salvation prayer. Of course, the questions were overly simplified. It became but a duty than a heart crying out to God for the lost. Our motivations must cut distinctively pure and not be lost in our affections.

# 6

## WORK OUT your SALVATION by Christian Living

*Make you perfect in every good work to do his will, working in*
*you that which is wellpleasing in his sight, through Jesus Christ;*
*to whom be glory for ever and ever. Amen.*
—Hebrews 13:21

*For it became him, for whom are all things, and by whom are*
*all things, in bringing many sons unto glory, to make the captain*
*of their salvation perfect through sufferings.*
—Hebrews 2:10.

Every Christian must be filled with the Holy Spirit in order to live and walk as a Christian, to conduct our lives in a manner that Christ has lived and given to us as examples, in the spirit of His person. Many today, like the disciples, have heard the call of Christ, and, like the disciples, have obeyed the call. And He has taught them, and He has breathed upon them, and they own Him sincerely as Saviour; yet, with all their allegiance to the Lord and all their trust in Jesus as Redeemer, they have never known that indwelling blessing of the Holy Spirit that makes a man in Christ a new creature. The Spirit never filled them; the Spirit never overwhelmed them, He never enthused in them the joy of saving grace, of their redemption. They have never made the living Christ a master of their lives. They have never felt themselves as empty vessels into which Christ was pouring grace and power. Hence their lives, however loyal and dutiful and however blessed in their willing service, are not the Christ-filled and Christ-empowered lives that are the peculiar creation of the Gospel. Have you been through this yourself, at some time in your Christian life, living a pretty much 'dead' life? I have. There was nothing of the energy of Christ, life simply a drudge. The light appeared to have gone out. But I did not stop there; I wanted more from the Lord. You would too. The Lord is always there to meet your faith in Him.

The indwelling of the Spirit is a privilege, an 'earnest' of our 'inheritance', a down payment God made in us that confirms we are His. God in giving us the Spirit graciously grants it as a part, a down payment, of our full inheritance. That earnest is a part of which every believer ought to claim. It is a blessing which every believer ought to have. Filled with and indwelt by the Holy Spirit, a Christian not only grows more and more able to die unto sin and to live unto righteousness, but also to grow in capacity for spiritual things—"*but be filled with the Spirit*" (Ephesians 5:18). The infilling of the Holy Spirit is constant to enable the heart and life of a Christian to grow and to enlarge, as his interests and knowledge expand to take in new territories of Christian experience.

God sent us the Word, He gave us His Word—His only begotten Son—to save us from His wrath, and He despatched His Holy Spirit to enable us to live as Christ lived, that we may bear fruit meet for the Kingdom of heaven. Abide therefore in Him; trust in Him for fruit and for life. *Abide in me, and I in you. As the branch cannot bear fruit of itself, except it abide in the vine; no more can ye, except ye abide in me. I am the vine, ye are the branches: He that abideth in me, and I in him, the same bringeth forth much fruit: for without me ye can do nothing.*—John 15:4-5.

**Prayer & Devotion:** Prayer is an act of man seeking relief from the fountain of God's mercy, and as used in the Bible have a simpler and a more complex, as well as a narrower and a wider representation. In the former case, it is supplication for benefits either for one's self (petition) or for others (intercession). In the latter, it is an act of worship that covers all souls in its approach to God, seeking His covering of grace for them. Supplication is at the heart of it, for prayer always springs out of a sense of need and a belief that God rewards them that diligently seek Him. *But without faith it is impossible to please him: for he that cometh to God must believe that he is, and that he is a rewarder of them that diligently seek him*—Hebrews 11:6. But adoration, confession, and thanksgiving also find in it a place, so that the supplicant becomes a worshipper. *Confess your faults one to another, and pray one for another, that ye may be healed. The effectual fervent prayer of a righteous man availeth much.*—James 5:16

> "For what have we to pray? Let me suggest to you the church, the ministry, your own soul, your children, your relations, your neighbours, your country, and the cause of God and truth throughout the world. Let us examine ourselves on this important matter."—*Spurgeon*

*Pray without ceasing.*—1 Thessalonians 5:17. *Rejoicing in hope; patient in tribulation; continuing instant in prayer.*—Romans 12:12. *Be careful for nothing; but in every thing by prayer and supplication with thanksgiving let your requests be made known unto God.*—Philippians 4:6. *Have we not all one father? Hath not one God created us? Why do we deal treacherously every man against his brother, by profaning the covenant of our fathers?*—Malachi 2:10.

> "Let us be diligent to keep the altar of private prayer burning. This is the very life of all piety. The sanctuary and family altars borrow their fires here, therefore let this burn without flickering. Secret devotion is the very essence, evidence, and measurement, of the vitality of our faith. Let your closet seasons be, if possible, regular, frequent, and undisturbed."—*Spurgeon*

*The fire shall ever be burning upon the altar; it shall never go out.*—Leviticus 6:13.

> "Do we engage with lukewarmness in private devotion? Is the fire of devotion burning dimly in our hearts? Do the chariot wheels drag heavily? Be alarmed; lukewarm devotion is the symptom of decay. Let us go with weeping, and ask for the Spirit of grace and of supplications. Let us set apart special seasons for extraordinary prayer. When this fire of devotion is smothered beneath the ashes of a worldly conformity, it will

dim the fire on the family altar, and lessen our influence both in the church and in the world."—*Spurgeon*

"The (fire ever burning upon the altar) will also apply to the altar of the heart. This is a golden altar indeed. God loves to see the hearts of his people glowing towards himself. Let us give to God our hearts, all blazing with love, and seek his grace, that the fire may never be quenched; it will not burn if the Lord does not keep it burning. Many foes will attempt to extinguish it; but if the unseen hand of God pours thereon the sacred oil, it will blaze higher and higher. Let us use texts of Scripture as fuel for our heart's fire; they are live coals. Let us attend sermons, but above all, let us be much alone with Jesus."—*Spurgeon*

Prayer is offering our desires to God. Prayer without desire is as a sacrifice without the fire of heaven to consume it. Our prayers are offered to God through the mediation of Christ. Let us look to Christ for how we should and should not pray. Principally, prayer is of the humble heart in secret, and not of the proud heart in appearance. *And when thou prayest, thou shalt not be as the hypocrites are: for they love to pray standing in the synagogues and in the corners of the streets, that they may be seen of men. Verily I say unto you, They have their reward. But thou, when thou prayest, enter into thy closet, and when thou hast shut thy door, pray to thy Father which is in secret; and thy Father which seeth in secret shall reward thee openly. But when ye pray, use not vain repetitions, as the heathen do: for they think that they shall be heard for their much speaking. Be not ye therefore like unto them: for your Father knoweth what things ye have need of, before ye ask him.* —Matthew6:5-8

Jesus gave us the best example of prayer and one that many of us have daily used, for its simplicity and for its all-embracing principles of worship. *After this manner therefore pray ye: Our Father which art in heaven, Hallowed be thy name. Thy kingdom come. Thy will be done in earth, as it is in heaven. Give us this day our daily bread. And forgive us our debts, as we forgive our debtors. And lead us not into temptation, but deliver us from evil: For thine is the kingdom, and the power, and the glory, forever. Amen.*—Matthew 6:9-13.

**Reading and Studying the Bible:** How am I to grow in my knowledge of Christ? The short answer is in the Word, and by the Word, through faith. How do I study the Bible? What are the fundamental tenets of my faith, of my belief in God? Another short answer is, to 'search the Scripture'.

Although addressed to Timothy, as the young pastor in his role, we may adduce from Paul's writing that it applies to believers in general. We may deduce that we are expected to show for 'study', quality strictly as God commands and reveals; quantity that comes with ceaseless earnest zeal and diligence; tried and tested unto God in preaching the gospel to unbelievers and in convicting the hearts of self and believers. *Study to shew thyself approved unto God, a workman that needeth not to be ashamed, rightly dividing the word of truth.*—2 Timothy 2:15.

We can assuredly dwell in the Word, Christ the Mediator of His church and His people, who abides in trust under God's shadow. *He that dwelleth in the secret place of the most High shall abide under the shadow of the Almighty. I will say of the LORD, He is my refuge and my fortress: my God; in him will I trust.*—Psalm 91:1-2

**Tithing and Love offering** is in gratitude to the Lord for His blessings. We ought to first set aside the tenth part of our takings, in salaries if in employment, or by way of profits if in business. Historically, since time immemorial, tithe was the custom of giving a tenth of the products/crops as of the seed of the land (Leviticus 27:30); oil and wine as of the fruits; and of the herd or the flock (Leviticus 27:32) or the spoils of war (1 Samuel 8:15, 17) to kings and priests. The Old Testament institutionalised tithing.

Tithing is thanksgiving. *Offer unto God thanksgiving; and pay thy vows unto the most High.*—Psalm 50:14. Jesus warns us about the attitude we should adopt in tithing. The love of God, justice, mercy, faith and all things holy and spiritual are more preferred than the ritual of giving. God looks for and after your heart, not mere duty. *Woe unto you, scribes and Pharisees, hypocrites! For ye pay tithe of mint and anise and cummin, and have omitted the weightier matters of the law, judgment, mercy, and faith: these ought ye to have done, and not to leave the other undone.*—Matthew 23:23.

**Saying grace** is an utterance of gratitude, a prayer of deep thankfulness at meal times for the food and drink that the Lord has provided as a means of physical sustenance. *And when he had thus spoken, he took bread, and gave thanks to God in presence of them all: and when he had broken it, he began to eat*—Acts 27:35. More than that is the spiritual life with which He has endued us. This attitude of gratitude expressed in our transformation in the new life in Christ is a gift of great value, liberally gifted to us by God's gracious favour. We are thankful for His continuing grace in giving us the Holy Spirit to guide and counsel us in wisdom, so that we are not comfortless. In the case of two or three at the table, we can be certain our Lord is in our midst enjoying our fellowship as we are immersed in His holy and loving presence. We 'say grace' not only for the material aspects of the partaking but significantly for the spiritual aspect of worship, and walking worthy in Him. *It is a good thing to give thanks unto the LORD, and to sing praises unto thy name, O most High.*—Psalm 92:1. *And Jesus took the loaves; and when he had given thanks, he distributed to the disciples, and the disciples to them that were set down; and likewise of the fishes as much as they would.*—John 6:11. *And whatsoever ye do in word or deed, do all in the name of the Lord Jesus, giving thanks to God and the Father by him.*—Colossians 3:17. *That ye would walk worthy of God, who hath called you unto his kingdom and glory.*—1 Thessalonians 2:12.

# 7

## Christian ministry is a Vocation

*"I am not what I ought to be, I am not what I want to be, I am not what I hope to be in another world—but still I am not what I once used to be, and by the grace of God I am what I am."*
—John Newton.

To what will I give my life ? Is it going to be to a career? Is it going to be to pleasure and entertainment? Is it going to be to amassing wealth? Or is it going to be to God's purpose? Even with these questions, a young Christian such as I could draw no clear line, as one unable to see the woods from the trees. It took a long while to see that the questions when better framed, draw us to the essence of all matters and issues. *Is God in my career? Is God in my pleasure and entertainment? Is God in my wealth? Is God in all my motivations? Is God in all that I do?*

Can I be in God's purpose when I vehemently pursue another such interested activity as a secular career or amassing wealth? Can I serve God and mammon? To these questions, we can ask, "Do I love God absolutely and despise mammon?" To love both is as schizophrenic, for each is characteristically at opposite poles, demanding from the pursuer a whole hearted devotion. *No man can serve two masters: for either he will hate the one, and love the other; or else he will hold to the one, and despise the other. Ye cannot serve God and mammon.*—Matthew 6:24.

Ministry has very extensive application within the New Testament and are by no means restricted to denote service within the Christian church; even when so restricted, the words are used in a great variety of meanings, for example,

1. Discipleship in general: *If any man serve me, let him follow me; and where I am, there shall also my servant be: if any man serve me, him will my Father honour.*—John 12:26;

2. Service rendered to the church because of the "gifts" bestowed: *or ministry, let us wait on our ministering: or he that teacheth, on teaching.*—Romans 12:7; (1Corinthians 12:5), and hence, all kinds of service: *then the twelve called the multitude of the disciples unto them, and said, It is not reason that we should leave the word of God, and serve tables.*—Acts 6:2; (Matthew 20:26);

3. Specifically the ministry of the Word—*for the perfecting of the saints, for the work of the ministry, for the edifying of the body of Christ* (Ephesians 4:12), and most frequently the 'apostleship'— *that I might finish my course with joy, and the ministry, which I have received of the Lord Jesus, to testify the gospel of the grace of God.* (Acts 20:24). (Acts 21:19; Romans 11:13);

4. Such services as feeding the poor: *And in those days, when the number of the disciples was multiplied, there arose a murmuring of the Grecians against the Hebrews, because their widows were neglected in the daily ministration*—Acts 6:1; (Acts 11:29; 12:25) or organizing and providing the great collection for the poor saints at Jerusalem (Romans 15:25; 2 Corinthians 8:4, 19).

5. Such services as those rendered by Stephanas: *I beseech you, brethren, (ye know the house of Stephanas, that it is the firstfruits of Achaia, and that they have addicted themselves to the ministry of the saints)*—1 Corinthians 16:15, by Archippus (Colossians 4:17), by Tychicus (Ephesians 6:21; Colossians 4:7), etc.

**Ushering** is a very important ministry in that ushers represent to worshippers as welcoming them to the house of God in Christian fellowship, and seeking to prepare the place of worship conducive for their hearts and minds to receive from the Word of God. In most churches, ushering is a well organised ministry of service, may thus well include song leading in praise and worship, and the corporate reading of the Word.

**Sunday school,** usually conducted before the worship service, is organised according to a logical grouping by age bands subject to the church size and composition. From these Sunday school classes, attendees receive and feed on the Word of God in a systematic approach to scripture so that they progress and mature doctrinally sound as Christians. Sunday school is not a substitute for personal study of Scripture and private/family devotions. Those must continue unabated to sanctify us for Christ's Kingdom.

**Missions:** Broadly, missions refer to persons sent to propagate the gospel, or evangelise the heathen. The societies for propagating the gospel have missions in almost every country. The motive of missions is a solemn and fearful responsibility. *For though I preach the gospel, I have nothing to glory of: for necessity is laid upon me; yea, woe is unto me, if I preach not the gospel! For if I do this thing willingly, I have a reward: but if against my will, a dispensation of the gospel is committed unto me.*—1 Corinthians 9:16-17. If a Christian does not show a genuine concern for the salvation of the lost, there can be no fruit of the Spirit in him—he may be still unregenerate. A Christianity that is non-missionary is not genuine. It would be most exemplary for one to go and where that is not possible, one must be willing to send others called to that ministry by way of material, financial, and prayer support. *For the love of Christ constraineth us; because we thus judge, that if one died for all, then were all dead.*—2 Corinthians 5:14.

The results of our labours in the Lord's work are contingent upon our efforts; not as in uncertainty but in that He has made them so. Whatever the difficulties and discouragements, we can always rely on His omnipotence to take us forward in joy and with confidence, knowing that His redemptive plan for all will not fail. Men who do their best always do more though haunted by the sense of failure. Stay true; be patient; be undaunted. Leave our usefulness for God to estimate. He will see to it that we do not live in vain. Many years ago, when in her early teens, my daughter at her primary school graduation valedictory speech encouraged those after her to 'do our best and God will do the rest': a simple but giant lesson in faith from a little young girl.

Does one need to grow? We must, for at conversion we were born again a new creature in Christ. We knew Him on paper, untested in the rubs of life. We now needed to know Him for real, in following His instructions,

His nature as He walked on earth as man, so that that our faith is in Him, brought to bear fully in the fiery trials and afflictions in our very own walk.

We work for God. *For none of us liveth to himself, and no man dieth to himself. For whether we live, we live unto the Lord; and whether we die, we die unto the Lord: whether we live therefore, or die, we are the Lord's.*—Romans 14:7-8.

We work for Christ. *Also I heard the voice of the Lord, saying, Whom shall I send, and who will go for us? Then said I, Here am I; send me.*—Isaiah 6:8.

We work for the souls of men. *Esteeming the reproach of Christ greater riches than the treasures in Egypt: for he had respect unto the recompence of the reward.*—Hebrews 11:26.

We are workers with God. *And they that be wise shall shine as the brightness of the firmament; and they that turn many to righteousness as the stars for ever and ever.*—Daniel 12:3. *We then, as workers together with him, beseech you also that ye receive not the grace of God in vain.*—2 Corinthians 6:1.

We are co-workers with Christ. *And when he is come, he will reprove the world of sin, and of righteousness, and of judgment: of sin, because they believe not on me; of righteousness, because I go to my Father, and ye see me no more; of judgment, because the prince of this world is judged.*—John 16:8-11.

We are fellow workers with the Holy Spirit His wise counsel and in obeying and thus performing God's will. His power flows in and through our lives

We also act in concert with angels. *But to which of the angels said he at any time, Sit on my right hand, until I make thine enemies thy footstool? Are they not all ministering spirits, sent forth to minister for them who shall be heirs of salvation?*—Hebrews 1:13-14. *And I said, Let them set a fair mitre upon his head. So they set a fair mitre upon his head, and clothed him with garments. And the angel of the LORD stood by. And the angel of the LORD protested unto Joshua, saying, thus saith the LORD of hosts; If thou wilt walk in my ways, and if thou wilt keep my charge, then thou shalt also judge my house, and shalt also keep my courts, and I will give thee places to walk among these that stand by.*—Zechariah 3:5-7.

41

Our ministry concur with all those who have gone before us as in the apostles, the martyrs, and others. Our ministry concur with those who are all godly people. *And I thank Christ Jesus our Lord, who hath enabled me, for that he counted me faithful, putting me into the ministry*—1Timothy 1:12. *Not that we are sufficient of ourselves to think any thing as of ourselves; but our sufficiency is of God. Who also hath made us able ministers of the new testament; not of the letter, but of the spirit: for the letter killeth, but the spirit giveth life.*—2 Corinthians 3:5-6.

Our ministry is totally dependent on Divine grace. Ministers and workers of God need prayers, intercessory prayers. *Who then is Paul, and who is Apollos, but ministers by whom ye believed, even as the Lord gave to every man? I have planted, Apollos watered; but God gave the increase. So then neither is he that planteth any thing, neither he that watereth; but God that giveth the increase.*—1 Corinthians 3:5-7. *But by the grace of God I am what I am: and his grace which was bestowed upon me was not in vain; but I laboured more abundantly than they all: yet not I, but the grace of God which was with me.*—1 Corinthians 15:10.

The Christian ministry of service is our work for Christ. Can we give anything short of our uttermost best? We cannot. Therefore, it is for us a vocation, a calling to serve in praise and honour of Him. The giving of ourselves wholeheartedly to the ministry of service for the Lord is a perquisite of the happy Christian life. We serve the Lord.

To be happy—to be serene and radiant—when the shadows deepen and the cross is heavy, is one of the finest of life's unconscious ministries. It is in such times of burden that one leans on and is heavily reliant on the Lord for strength and deliverance. The clouds of gloom seem to stubbornly follow us overhead. In such an attitude, one becomes of great service to all about him, setting a Christian example of faith in the Lord, trusting fully in His providence in spite of the shadows of gloom and an unrelenting yoke. *Servants, obey in all things your masters according to the flesh; not with eyeservice, as menpleasers; but in singleness of heart, fearing God: And whatsoever ye do, do it heartily, as to the Lord, and not unto men: Knowing that of the Lord ye shall receive the reward of the inheritance: for ye serve the Lord Christ.*—Colossians 3:22-24.

## **Notes**

"It is sometimes very difficult not to be offended in Jesus Christ. The offences may be circumstantial. I find myself in a prison-house—a narrow sphere, a sick chamber, an unpopular position—when I had hoped for wide opportunities. Yes, but He knows what is best for me. My environment is of His determining. He means it to intensify my faith, to draw me into nearer communion with Himself, to ripen my power. In the dungeon my soul should prosper.

The offence may be mental. I am haunted by perplexities, questions, which I cannot solve. I had hoped that, when I gave myself to Him, my sky would always be clear; but often it is overspread by mist and cloud. Yet, let me believe that, if difficulties remain, it is that I may learn to trust Him all the more implicitly—to trust and not be afraid. Yes, and by my intellectual conflicts, I am trained to be a tutor to other storm-driven men.

The offence may be spiritual. I had fancied that within His fold I should never feel the biting winds of temptation; but it is best as it is. His grace is magnified. My own character is matured. His Heaven is sweeter at the close of the day. There I shall look back on the turnings and trials of the way, and shall sing the praises of my Guide. So, let come what will come, His will is welcome; and I shall refuse to be offended in my loving Lord."—*Alexander Smellie*

*"Blessed is he, whosoever shall not be offended in me" (Luke 7:23).*

# 8

## Do we need Theology?

*"If ye know these things, happy are ye if ye do them."*
—John 13:17

*"Be ye doers of the word, and not hearers only, deceiving your own selves."*
—James 1:22

What is theology? It sounds like you need to study a degree course to 'get' it. Can that be the case? It appears complex. Where is the simplicity I saw in Christ when I read the gospels? The first church to which I went hardly taught and I hardly studied doctrine. The focus was significantly on what to do and not to do, how Christians should conduct themselves, that one needed time and again, to ask God to fill one with the Holy Spirit as though they had never been filled with the Holy Spirit of God. It was confusing as I thought we all had the Spirit dwell in us at the time we called upon Christ's name in confession of our sins, our sinful nature, turned away from them and looked to Christ for our salvation. The feeling was that if I did not speak in tongue, then I did not have the Spirit. Understanding the Holy Spirit, the third Person in the Triune God, appeared to me as fundamental and natural for a Christian, yet I was baffled with different answers from different quarters. There was too much of feelings, opinions, preferences, and emotions. This is where doctrine becomes necessarily important as it objectively draws from Scripture and exposes the person of God as revealed therein. This enables the student of the Bible to not lean on his own relative understanding or subjective feelings but to systematically lean on Scripture to receive instruction, and to rightly divide the word of truth. *Study to shew thyself approved unto God, a workman that needeth not to be ashamed, rightly dividing the word of truth.*—2 Timothy 2:15.

The term 'theology' is derived from two Greek words, *theos* for God, and *logos* for a discourse. Literally, theology means 'a discourse concerning God'. *Theology*, in its modern understanding, is that science which treats of the existence, the character, and the attributes of God; his laws and government; the doctrines that we are to believe, the moral change that we must experience, and the duties that we are required to perform. In this sense, *theology* embraces the whole system of revealed religion and at the same time, signifying learned or scientific instruction respecting God. Hence, a *theologian* is one who is able thoroughly to explain, prove, and defend the doctrines of religion, and to teach them to others.

Theology in embracing the whole system of revealed religion, does not intend to convey the idea that *theology* and *religion* are terms of precisely the same import; for though they should not be employed in opposition to each other, yet they differ materially in regard to their signification. *Religion*, understood *subjectively* and in its most comprehensive sense, includes:

1.  Knowledge of God in regard to his nature, his attributes, his relations to men, and his will with respect to them.
2.  Affections, and conduct, that correspond to the knowledge of God.

The former concerns the *theory* of religion, and addresses to the human understanding; while the latter, the *practical* part, belongs to the will and affections. These are two essential parts of religion always united in the teachings of Christ and his apostles. *"If ye know these things, happy are ye if ye do them."* (John 13:17). *"Be ye doers of the word, and not hearers only, deceiving your own selves."* (James 1:22). Religion, in this sense of the term, comprehends theology, as a system of doctrines, and also practical piety.

# 9

## Scripture defines Doctrine

*They also that erred in spirit shall come to understanding, and
they that murmured shall learn doctrine.*
—Isaiah 29:24.

What is Christian doctrine and precepts? We generally have the idea that doctrine is quite beyond our comprehension, apart from our untrained mind, and is not something we use or talk about in the daily conduct of life. However, we do know also that practical Christian living cannot stand apart from Biblical teaching and knowledge. Christians must have a sound and strong foundation built and settled on the truths of God's Word. The earliest teaching of the apostles consisted essentially of three propositions, that:

(a) Jesus was the Christ (Acts 3:18);
(b) He was risen from the dead (Acts 1:22; Acts 2:24, 32); and
(c) Salvation was by faith in His name (Acts 2:38; 3:16).

In the original languages, doctrine is 'what is received'. *My doctrine shall drop as the rain, my speech shall distil as the dew, as the small rain upon the tender herb, and as the showers upon the grass: Because I will publish the name of the LORD: ascribe ye greatness unto our God.*—Deuteronomy 32:2-3.

In the general and pastoral epistles in the New Testament, it appears as *a body of teaching* generally accepted as sound doctrine that had emerged following Christ's resurrection. The faith had become a body of truth *'which was once delivered unto the saints'.*—Jude 1:3. Hence, doctrine became 'the matter taught'. **All believers must receive instruction in doctrine** and we cannot assume lightly, such a need for instruction; doctrine is as the cement/glue that joins the stones in the building of the church of Christ. Many points in Scripture are things that tend to good and sound doctrine for a firm foundation in church-building. *For whoremongers, for them that defile themselves with mankind, for menstealers, for liars, for perjured persons, and if there be any other thing that is contrary to sound doctrine*—1Timothy 1:10. *If any man teach otherwise, and consent not to wholesome words, even the words of our Lord Jesus Christ, and to the doctrine which is according to godliness.*—1Timothy 6:3. *Hold fast the form of sound words, which thou hast heard of me, in faith and love which is in Christ Jesus.*—2 Timothy 1:13. *For the time will come when they will not endure sound doctrine; but after their own lusts shall they heap to themselves teachers, having itching ears; and they shall turn away their ears from the truth, and shall be turned unto fables.*—2Timothy 4:3. *Holding fast the faithful word as he hath been taught, that he may be able by sound doctrine both to exhort and to convince the gainsayers.*—Titus 1:9. *But speak thou the things which become sound doctrine.*—Titus 2:1. *If thou put the brethren in remembrance of these things, thou shalt be a good minister of Jesus Christ, nourished up in the words of faith and of good doctrine, whereunto thou hast attained.*—1Timothy 4:6.

What the Law cannot do in delivering us from sin, God does through Christ. *For what the law could not do, in that it was weak through the flesh, God sending his own Son in the likeness of sinful flesh, and for sin, condemned sin in the flesh: That the righteousness of the law might be fulfilled in us, who walk not after the flesh, but after the Spirit.*—Romans 8:3-4.

John Owen, a puritan divine, treats doctrine—though not called by that name here—as things that guide the mind and conscience of the Christian believer, centred about the foundation of his salvation, giving him instruction in the truth, allowing him to understand the mysteries of the gospel as God reveals them, and so establishing his mind in the Lord.

"More weight is to be put on the steady guidance of the mind and conscience of one believer, really exercised about the foundation of his peace and acceptance with God, than on the confutation of ten wrangling disputers . . . to declare and vindicate the truth unto the instruction and edification of such as love it in sincerity, to extricate their minds from those difficulties in this particular instance, which some endeavour to cast on all Gospel mysteries, to direct the consciences of them that inquire after abiding peace with God, and to establish the minds of them that do believe, are the things I have aimed at."—*John Owen*

Theologian Arthur Pink sets Doctrinal Christianity side by side with Practical Christianity; the former designed to enlighten, instruct, and inform through principle. The latter is driven by principles set out in the former, and tends to good works.

"Doctrinal preaching is designed to enlighten the understanding, to instruct the mind, to inform the judgment. It is that which supplies motives to gratitude and furnishes incentives to good works. Doctrinal Christianity is both the ground and the motive of practical Christianity, for it is *principle* and not *emotion* or impulse which is the dynamic of the spiritual life . . . There is no doctrine revealed in Scripture for a merely speculative knowledge, but all is to exert a powerful influence upon conduct. God's design in all that He has revealed to us is to the purifying of our affections and the transforming of our characters."—*Arthur W. Pink.*

Let us note what is in Scripture about the source of doctrine. It is from Scripture inspired of God that doctrine is drawn. *All scripture is given by inspiration of God, and is profitable for doctrine, for reproof, for correction, for instruction in righteousness.*—2 Timothy 3:16

### <u>Notes</u>

These notes intended not as studies, are hence brief, in order that readers may concern themselves with these terms in their simplest form possible for understanding. The author is not a theologian, just a common lay disciple of Christ who had sought to understand them over time and had found doctrine or things that become sound doctrine to be of immense value for all believers as being fundamental to our faith in Christ. Readers desiring the deeper truths of God's Word are encouraged to pursue a systematic extended programme or to embark on seriously committed guided self study.

**Depravity**

Depravity, more commonly, total depravity, is not so much of man's conduct or behaviour. It is really about man's state or condition. The human soul is essentially under sin. In that state, he is under sin. *And this I say, that the covenant, that was confirmed before of God in Christ, the law, which was four hundred and thirty years after, cannot disannul, that it should make the promise of none effect. For if the inheritance be of the law, it is no more of promise: but God gave it to Abraham by promise. Wherefore then serveth the law? It was added because of transgressions, till the seed should come to whom the promise was made; and it was ordained by angels in the hand of a mediator. Now a mediator is not a mediator of one, but God is one. Is the law then against the promises of God? God forbid: for if there had been a law given which could have given life, verily righteousness should have been by the law. But the scripture hath concluded all under sin, that the promise by faith of Jesus Christ might be given to them that believe. But before faith came, we were kept under the law, shut up unto the faith which should afterwards be revealed. Wherefore the law was our schoolmaster to bring us unto Christ, that we might be justified by faith.*—Galatians 3.17-24.

There are 3 aspects of sin:

(a) <u>Personal sin</u> that comes from acts of the individual, a manifestation of the exercise of his will. *For all have sinned, and come short of the glory of God*—Romans 3.23. Man ends up with transgression such as overstepping his bounds, sidestepping God's out-of-bound markers. Other words used in the Bible include error, disobedience, unbelief, lawlessness, ungodliness, wickedness, sin, iniquity, and evil.

(b) <u>The depraved nature produces the sinful act</u>. Adam by his disobedience changed from untried innocence to a nature confirmed in sin. Adam was corrupted; his fruit bore the corruption of that root. *For the law of the Spirit of life in Christ Jesus hath made me free from the law of sin and death.*—Romans 8:2. (See also Romans 7:25; 3:10-18; Galatians 5:19-21).

(c) <u>Man placed by God in a state of sin</u> is not only guilty of personal sin but harbours in his heart the sin nature. When man was in the Garden of Eden, fellowship with God was possible. He was in a righteous world and could obtain righteousness. However, when he disobeyed God, his wayward nature no longer was in harmony with the righteous world of God. He had practised sin when he acted against God's instruction. Now he was also a sinner by nature. *But the scripture hath concluded all under sin, that the promise by faith of Jesus Christ might be given to them that believe.*— Galatians 3:22.

Man is placed in a state of sin, under sin. *What then? Are we better than they? No, in no wise: for we have before proved both Jews and Gentiles, that they are all under sin; as it is written, There is none righteous, no, not one.*— Romans 3:9-10.

Man is spiritually dead. *And you hath he quickened, who were dead in trespasses and sins.*—Ephesians 2:1. *Behold, all souls are mine; as the soul of the father, so also the soul of the son is mine: the soul that sinneth, it shall die.*—Ezekiel 18:4. *For the wages of sin is death; but the gift of God is eternal life through Jesus Christ our Lord.*—Romans 6:23. *Wherefore, as by one man sin entered into the world, and death by sin; and so death passed upon all men, for that all have sinned: (For until the law sin was in the world: but sin is not imputed when there is no law.*—Romans 5:12

He is also under condemnation. *He that believeth on him is not condemned: but he that believeth not is condemned already, because he hath not believed in the name of the only begotten Son of God.*—John 3:18. *He that believeth on the Son hath everlasting life: and he that believeth not the Son shall not see life; but the wrath of God abideth on him.*—John 3:36. *For the wrath of God is revealed from heaven against all ungodliness and unrighteousness of men, who hold the truth in unrighteousness.*—Romans 1:18. *For God hath not appointed us to wrath, but to obtain salvation by our Lord Jesus Christ, who died for us, that, whether we wake or sleep, we should live together with him.*—1 Thessalonians 5:9. *Who shall be punished with everlasting destruction from the presence of the Lord, and from the glory of his power.*—2 Thessalonians 1:9

Man is under the power of Satan. *And we know that we are of God, and the whole world lieth in wickedness.*—1 John 5:19. *In whom the god of this world hath blinded the minds of them which believe not, lest the light of the glorious gospel of Christ, who is the image of God, should shine unto them.*—2 Corinthians 4:4. *Wherein in time past ye walked according to the course of this world, according to the prince of the power of the air, the spirit that now worketh in the children of disobedience: among whom also we all had our conversation in times past in the lusts of our flesh, fulfilling the desires of the flesh and of the mind; and were by nature the children of wrath, even as others.*—Ephesians 2:1-3. *Who hath delivered us from the power of darkness, and hath translated us into the kingdom of his dear Son.*—Colossians 1:13.

In summary, man in his natural state is **lost**. In the 15th chapter of the gospel according to Luke, the three parables spoken of express the lost state of man: the sheep that was lost, the coin that was lost, and the (prodigal) son that was lost.

The only answer to the depravity of man is Christ by God's redeeming grace, not a physical church, not the ordinances, not good works. We are under sin by a natural birth; by a new birth, we are placed in Christ Jesus. Our old nature that was in Adam was under sin; it is now placed in Christ. The man who was under condemnation now has the promise. *But the scripture hath concluded all under sin, that the promise by faith of Jesus Christ might be given to them that believe.*—Romans 8:1.

## Grace

1. Grace is God's *answer* to man's helplessness under sin.
2. Grace is Divine *gift*. It is something we cannot, out of ourselves, work out. It is given in God's good pleasure and in His favour to us.
3. Grace *is received* out of God's mercy and is not something we accept out of our own will. God drew us into the light and we saw His righteousness and our own depraved nature. We receive grace out of God's abundant mercy. Perhaps this will become clearer when we get to Repentance and Faith.

Common grace (not a term in scripture) is given to all, believer and non-believer. It reveals God's *love* for His creation. *Who in times past suffered all nations to walk in their own ways. Nevertheless he left not himself without witness, in that he did good, and gave us rain from heaven, and fruitful seasons, filling our hearts with food and gladness.*—Acts 14:16-17 Special or saving (not a term in scripture) grace is given to those in whom He did foreknow, predestined, and *called* (Romans 8:30).

4.  Grace in us is *manifested* through various means and/or manifestations, in our walk and conduct in life, by word, deed, and thought. We are shaped with the Divine character of God the Father, Christ His Son, and the indwelling Holy Spirit that we are compelled, in our union with Him, to manifest His grace through works in faith. The Holy Spirit works *by* us, not *for* us.

## Faith

Faith is the link between our souls and God. It is the capacity of entering into fellowship with the eternal Love and Power, so that we are able to do all things with the sense that it is not we who do them, but God in us and with us. Faith is the open door and window towards God. In faith, our heart goes out towards God in clinging dependence, and God comes in to strengthen us with His Divine fullness. Faith is reliance and trust in and towards God, Who is all trustworthy, *great is Thy faithfulness*. In Hebrews 11, all the accounts of those who acted in faith of old times did them all in simple reliance and obedience to God. Faith is not the power that leads us to victories. Faith is the power that protects us in battle. *For whatsoever is born of God overcometh the world: and this is the victory that overcometh the world, even our faith.*
—1 John 5:4.

Faith is simply reliance upon the word, power, love, of God; it is precisely that which, on man's side, *adjusts him* to the living and merciful presence and action of a trusted God. Faith, in its nature, not by any mere arbitrary arrangement, is man's one possible receptive attitude, that in which he brings nothing as he comes before God in complete humility, so that he may receive all from the saving grace in Christ's redemptive work on the cross. Thus, faith is our side of union with Christ; *faith is our means of possessing all His benefits, pardon, justification, purification, life, peace, glory.*

**Faith communicates our trust and reliance in God** without which we cannot be saved. Faith is the principal saving grace; and unbelief the chief damning sin. *He that believeth and is baptized shall be saved; but he that believeth not shall be damned.*—Mark 16:16.

God bears a witness to all who trust Him. He never fails us in the hour of need. His response is the echo of our appeal. So ***God answers faith.*** Paul spells out in specific terms how our salvation is accomplished. We learn that *all have sinned and fall short of the glory of God.*—Romans 3:23. We also discover that *God demonstrates His own love toward us, in that while we were still sinners, Christ died for us.*—Romans 5:8. *Sin entered into the world, and death by sin* (through Adam) *and so death passed upon all men; for that all have sinned* (Romans 5:12). But salvation is offered to all through God as the Son of man, Jesus Christ. We can escape eternal death by trusting in Christ as our Redeemer.

We may have true faith but faith untested is little faith, having little strength and is weak. The living out of faith is in trials, tried and tested for God's praise, honour and glory. **Tried faith gives experience**, experience of God's strength, an evidence of our weakness, and that He is ever faithful (Hebrews 10:23) to watch over and calm the storm, to succour us when the worst is at hand. Hence, take comfort in trials, they are *purposeful*, that God is *in our midst*, for our *faith is more precious than gold* that perishes. The trial of our faith is precious too. *That the trial of your faith, being much more precious than of gold that perisheth, though it be tried with fire, might be found unto praise and honour and glory at the appearing of Jesus Christ:*—1 Peter 1:7

## Repentance

In the Old Testament context, the definition of repentance was to pant, to sigh, to groan, to lament, or to grieve. Another meaning is to turn, to return. They express the twofold idea of grief, and the altered relation following the grief. Simply, it is translated by 'repent' and 'return'.

In the New Testament usage, it means to care, be concerned, a feeling of care, concern or regret. One can repent in the sense of regret or remorse, and not consider an abandonment of sin. A *second* meaning is to change the mind, as in a spiritual change implied in a return to God. One changes the opinion of or purpose with regard to sin. As a vital and essential experience at conversion, repentance is to manifest its reality by producing good fruits appropriate to the new spiritual life (Matthew 3:8). A *third* meaning is to turn over, to turn upon, and to turn unto. It expresses the positive side of a change involved in New Testament repentance, or to indicate the *return to God* of which the *turning from sin* is the negative aspect. The two conceptions are inseparable and complementary. The word is used to express the spiritual transition from sin to God: *and all that dwelt at Lydda and Saron saw him, and turned to the Lord.*—Acts 9:35; *For they themselves shew of us what manner of entering in we had unto you, and how ye turned to God from idols to serve the living and true God*—1 Thessalonians 1:9; to strengthen the idea of faith *And the hand of the Lord was with them: and a great number believed, and turned unto the Lord.*—Acts 11:21; and to complete and emphasise the change required by the New Testament *But shewed first unto them of Damascus, and at Jerusalem, and throughout all the coasts of Judaea, and then to the Gentiles, that they should repent and turn to God, and do works meet for repentance.*—Acts 26:20.

Dominant in repentance is therefore, *a change of the sinner's mind*, with accompanying grief and consequent reformation, a turning from his evil ways and live. The change wrought in repentance is deep and radical as to affect the whole spiritual nature and to involve the entire personality, wherein the *intellect functions*, the *emotions aroused*, and the *will moved* to act out the change.

Man must apprehend sin as unutterably heinous, the divine law as perfect and inexorable, and he falls short or falls below the requirements of a holy God (Job 42:5-6; Psalm 51:3). *Therefore by the deeds of the law there shall no flesh be justified in his sight: for by the law is the knowledge of sin*—Romans 3:20.

There is a type of grief that results in repentance, and another which plunges into remorse. There is therefore, a godly sorrow and also a sorrow of the world. The former brings life; the latter, death. *Now I rejoice, not that ye were made sorry, but that ye sorrowed to repentance: for ye were made sorry after a godly manner, that ye might receive damage by us in nothing. For godly sorrow worketh repentance to salvation not to be repented of: but the sorrow of the world worketh death.*—2 Corinthians 7:9-10. *Then Judas, which had betrayed him, when he saw that he was condemned, repented himself, and brought again the thirty pieces of silver to the chief priests and elders, Saying, I have sinned in that I have betrayed the innocent blood. And they said, what is that to us? see thou to that. And he cast down the pieces of silver in the temple, and departed, and went and hanged himself.*—Matthew 27:3; Luke 18:23. There must be a consciousness of sin in its effect on man and in its relation to God, before there can be a hearty turning away from unrighteousness. The feeling naturally accompanying repentance implies a conviction of personal sin and sinfulness and an earnest appeal to God to forgive according to His mercy. *Have mercy upon me, O God, according to thy lovingkindness: according unto the multitude of thy tender mercies blot out my transgressions. Wash me throughly from mine iniquity, and cleanse me from my sin.*—Psalm 51:1-2; (Psalm 51:10-14).

The demand for repentance implies free will and individual responsibility. That men are called upon to repent there can be no doubt, and that God as taking the initiative in repentance is equally clear. Repentance as to its nature is a gift of God and at the same time a duty of man. *When they heard these things, they held their peace, and glorified God, saying, Then hath God also to the Gentiles granted repentance unto life.*—Acts 11:18. The solution of the problem belongs to the spiritual sphere. There can be no external substitute for the internal change. Sackcloth and ash for the body as in times of old, and remorse for the soul, are not to be confused with a determined abandonment of sin and return to God. Not material sacrifice, but a spiritual change, is the inexorable demand of God in both the old and new dispensations. *The sacrifices of God are a broken spirit: a broken and a contrite heart, O God, thou wilt not despise.*—Psalm 51:17; *to what purpose is the multitude of your sacrifices unto me? Saith the LORD: I am full of the burnt offerings of rams, and the fat of fed beasts; and I delight not in the blood of bullocks, or of lambs, or of he goats.*—Isaiah 1:11; *to what purpose cometh there to me incense from Sheba, and the sweet cane from a far country? Your burnt offerings are not acceptable, nor your sacrifices sweet unto me.*—Jeremiah 6:20; *for I desired mercy, and not sacrifice; and the knowledge of God more than burnt offerings.*—Hosea 6:6

## Regeneration

We may all be as Nicodemus, puzzled at how anyone can be born again. . . . *Jesus answered and said unto him, Verily, verily, I say unto thee, except a man be born again, he cannot see the kingdom of God. Nicodemus saith unto him, How can a man be born when he is old? Can he enter the second time into his mother's womb, and be born? . . .* —John 3:1-8. Jesus' reply was that "except a man be born of water and *of* the Spirit, he cannot enter into the kingdom of God. That which is born of the flesh is flesh; and that which is born of the Spirit is spirit." The wind blows where it lists, and we hear the sound but cannot tell when and where it comes, and where it goes: so is every one that is born of the Spirit. Words used in the Bible include: 'to have a new heart', 'to be a new creature', 'to pass from death unto life', 'to walk in the light', 'to be born of God', 'to be born of the Spirit'. A sinner cannot be regenerated if there is no change in his moral character. A regenerated man comes about by an act of Divine agency in making the sinner holy; if no such change has taken place, then the Divine agency was not at work in making the sinner holy, thus he cannot be regenerated.

What comes first, repentance or regeneration? In every instance of the verses provided below, it becomes evident that repentance must clearly take precedence to a man's regeneration. Only after a man has repented, has changed from a sinner's mind, accompanied by grief and reformation, to turn to righteousness, that regeneration is effected by the Holy Spirit. . . . *Except ye repent, ye shall all likewise perish.*—Luke 13:3; *and they went out, and preached that men should repent.*—Mark 6:12; *Then Peter said unto them, Repent, and be baptized every one of you in the name of Jesus Christ for the remission of sins, and ye shall receive the gift of the Holy Ghost.*—Acts 2:38; *Repent ye therefore, and be converted, that your sins may be blotted out, when the times of refreshing shall come from the presence of the Lord.*—Acts 3:19; *And the times of this ignorance God winked at; but now commandeth all men every where to repent.*—Acts 17:30.

## Imputation

Imputation, is the act of imputing or charging; attribution; generally in an ill sense; as the imputation of crimes of faults to the true authors of them. We are liable to the imputation or numerous sins and errors, to the imputation of pride, vanity, and self-confidence; to the imputation of weakness and irresolution, or of rashness.

To impute something means "to apply something to your account." The Bible teaches that no one can earn salvation. However, God will give it to us freely if we have faith in Him. God honours the attitude of our hearts and imputes righteousness to our accounts. To be able to impute righteousness to those living during Old Testament times, God looked ahead to the work of Christ on the cross. Now He looks back to the Cross. But in both cases, God's people have been saved by grace through faith. *God imputeth righteousness without works, Saying, Blessed are they whose iniquities are forgiven, and whose sins are covered. Blessed is the man to whom the Lord will not impute sin.*—Romans 4

To impute is to count, to esteem, to reckon, to charge to one's account, whether a good deed for reward. *Then stood up Phinehas, and executed judgment: and so the plague was stayed. And that was counted unto him for righteousness unto all generations for evermore* (Psalm 106:30); or a bad deed for punishment. *And bringeth it not unto the door of the tabernacle of the congregation, to offer an offering unto the LORD before the tabernacle of the LORD; blood shall be imputed unto that man; he hath shed blood; and that man shall be cut off from among his people* (Leviticus 17:4). It makes no difference whether prior to the imputation that which is imputed is something personally one's own, as in the case where his own good deed was imputed to Phinehas (Psalm 106:30ff); or something which is not personally one's own, as where Paul asks that a debt not personally his own be charged to him. *If he hath wronged thee, or oweth thee ought, put that on mine account* (Philemon 1:18).

In all these cases, the act of imputation is simply the charging of one with something. It denotes just what we mean by our ordinary use of the term. *It does not change the inward state or character of the person to whom something is imputed.*

Three acts of imputation are given special prominence in the Scripture, and are implicated in the Scriptural doctrines of Original Sin, Atonement and Justification, though not usually expressed by the words.

### Original sin
Original sin, as applied to Adam, was his first act of *disobedience* in eating the forbidden fruit; as applied to his posterity, it is understood to mean

either the sin of Adam imputed to his posterity, or that corruption of nature, or total depravity, which has been derived from him in consequence of his falling away, his apostasy.

In strictness, original sin is an improper use of words, as sin implies volition and the transgression of a known rule of duty by a moral agent. But this application of the words has been established by long use, and it serves to express ideas which many wise and good men think on this subject.

**Atonement**

The word means agreement; concord; reconciliation, after an enmity or a controversy. The English word is derived from the Hebrew word meaning 'cover' of the Ark of the Covenant, constituted as the mercy seat. Atonement therefore means reconciliation to favour, or more specifically the means or conditions of reconciliation to favour. *For scarcely for a righteous man will one die: yet peradventure for a good man some would even dare to die. But God commendeth his love toward us, in that, while we were yet sinners, Christ died for us. Much more then, being now justified by his blood, we shall be saved from wrath through him. For if, when we were enemies, we were reconciled to God by the death of his Son, much more, being reconciled, we shall be saved by his life.*—Romans 5:7-10

Expiation; satisfaction or reparation made by giving an equivalent for an injury, or by doing or suffering that which is received in satisfaction for an offense or injury; with for. *And Moses said to Aaron, go to the altar, and offer thy sin-offering, and thy burnt-offering, and make an atonement for thyself and for the people.*—Leviticus 9:7

In theology, atonement is the expiation of sin made by the obedience and personal sufferings of Christ. This, we can better understand by addressing the letter and the spirit of God's moral law. The *letter of the law* is inexorable; it condemns and sentences to death all violators of its precepts, without regard to atonement or repentance. The letter of the law is found in precepts and commandments (as in the Decalogue) that governs outward acts. The *spirit of moral law*, however, allows and requires that upon condition of satisfaction being made to public justice, and the return of the sinner to obedience, he shall live and not die. The spirit of the moral law requires disinterested benevolence that may be expressed in one word—love, the Love of God.

## Justification

Justification by faith is illustrated in the Old Testament through the lives of Abraham and David. The preceding section on atonement adds clarity to justification with regard to functioning of the moral law. *If there be a controversy between men, and they come unto judgment, that the judges may judge them; then they shall justify the righteous, and condemn the wicked.*— Deuteronomy 25:1. This principle given to man to regulate their affairs is also one by which God administers justice. Therefore when a holy and righteous God sits in judgement to dispense, He must pronounce the world guilty. How will man be saved? How will God, also a loving and compassionate God full of mercy and grace save man? God must acquit or justify the righteous and at the same time condemn the guilty. Justification then is the divine pronouncement that the man in Christ Jesus is fully acceptable to God Himself. God removes the sin, cancels our indebtedness, and places us in Christ Jesus as a new creation. God gives for our possession, the righteousness of Christ; that we can come before the Judge to be examined and be acquitted on the fact of Jesus Christ.

## Substitution

This designates the scriptural doctrine of the atonement, in that Christ died for our sins in our place as our substitute. The moral order and the necessity for satisfying its demands together with the necessity of penalty for the vindication of the moral order speak of substitution.

## Redemption

To redeem means to tear loose, to rescue, or to purchase from a ransom. Money is paid according to law to buy back something which must be delivered or rescued (Numbers 3:51; Nehemiah 5:8).

In the New Testament the idea of redemption has more a suggestion of ransom. Men are held under the curse of the law (Galatians 3:13), or of sin itself (Romans 7:23 f). The Redeemer purchases their deliverance by offering Himself as payment for their redemption (Ephesians 1:7; 1Peter 1:18). The man redeemed by money payment is freed from the dark prison to the light of day, or he comes out of slavery into freedom, or he is restored to his home and friends. The man under the law is redeemed from the burden and curse of the law.

The aim of redemption, to beget in men's hearts the will to do right, and once fulfilled, leads them to seek successfully along all possible avenues for life. This, of course, does not mean that the redeemed life gives itself up to development of itself toward higher excellences. It means that the redeemed life is delivered from every form of selfishness. In the unselfish seeking of life for others the redeemed life finds its own greatest achievement and happiness. *For whosoever will save his life shall lose it: and whosoever will lose his life for my sake shall find it.*—Matthew 16:25

### Reconciliation

The great doctrine is the reconciliation of God and men. The word 'to reconcile' means literally to exchange, to bring into a changed relationship. Some maintain that it is only a change in the sinner that is intended, a laying aside of his enmity, and coming into peaceful relations with God. But that manifestly does not exhaust the meaning, nor is it in the great Pauline passages the primary and dominant meaning.

The essence of the gospel is found in the propitiatory death of the Lord Jesus Christ, *being justified freely by his grace through the redemption that is in Christ Jesus: Whom God hath set forth to be a propitiation through faith in his blood, to declare his righteousness for the remission of sins that are past, through the forbearance of God; To declare, I say, at this time his righteousness: that he might be just, and the justifier of him which believeth in Jesus.*—Romans 3:24-26), through whom alone can men who have been *brought under the judgment of God* (Romans 3:19) find justification, salvation, deliverance from the wrath of God, *but for us also, to whom it shall be imputed, if we believe on him that raised up Jesus our Lord from the dead; who was delivered for our offences, and was raised again for our justification.* (Romans 4:25-26; 5:1-6). It is the settled opposition of His holy nature against sin.

Reconciliation is God-ward, as Well as Man-ward: *For if, while we were enemies, we were reconciled to God through the death of his Son, much more, being reconciled, shall we be saved by his life.*—Romans 5:10

God has set aside His holy opposition to the sinner, and shows Him willing to bring men into peace with Himself. He has found satisfaction in that great work of His Son; has been reconciled, and now calls upon men to be reconciled to Him—to receive the reconciliation.

## Propitiation

It is inconceivable that man fallen from Adam's sin and his own by his fallen nature, could in any way compensate for human sin, or could offer any vindication of the moral order of God's universe. The natural man, when convicted by the Holy Spirit of God, may recognise the rightness of God's law and may earnestly wish to be in harmony with it, but the natural man stands utterly in need of both *propitiation* whereby he may be justified, and *enablement* whereby he may begin and continue to live a holy life. (1 John 2:2; 4:10; Romans 3:25). The propitiation originates with God, not to appease Himself, but to justify Himself in His uniform kindness to men deserving of judgement and harshness.

## Sanctification

The word means 'being made holy'. To sanctify is to set apart to a holy use—to willingly consecrate a thing to the service of God. This is plainly both the Old and the New Testament use of the term. Essentially, it is separation from relationships contrary to God's will, unto relationships harmonious with God's will. It speaks of a love for God, of entire obedience to the moral law.

1. It is a work of the Spirit. *For, brethren, ye have been called unto liberty; only use not liberty for an occasion to the flesh, but by love serve one another (v13). For all the law is fulfilled in one word, even in this; Thou shalt love thy neighbour as thyself (v14). This I say then, Walk in the Spirit, and ye shall not fulfil the lust of the flesh (v16). For the flesh lusteth against the Spirit, and the Spirit against the flesh: and these are contrary the one to the other: so that ye cannot do the things that ye would (v17). But if ye be led of the Spirit, ye are not under the law (v18). Of the which I tell you before, as I have also told you in time past, that they which do such things shall not inherit the kingdom of God (v21). But the fruit of the Spirit is love, joy, peace, longsuffering, gentleness, goodness, faith, Meekness, temperance: against such there is no law. And they that are Christ's have crucified the flesh with the*

*affections and lusts. If we live in the Spirit, let us also walk in the Spirit. Let us not be desirous of vain glory, provoking one another, envying one another (v23-26).*—Galatians 5:13-26.

2. It is holy living. *Mortify therefore your members which are upon the earth; fornication, uncleanness, inordinate affection, evil concupiscence, and covetousness, which is idolatry: For which things' sake the wrath of God cometh on the children of disobedience*—Colossians 3:5-6 (also Ephesians 4:24-25).

3. It is against perfectionism. *Beloved, now are we the sons of God, and it doth not yet appear what we shall be: but we know that, when he shall appear, we shall be like him; for we shall see him as he is*—1 John 3:2.

## Preservation

Preservation shares the same concept as security, and denotes a special persistency, the undying continuance of the new life (manifested in faith and holiness) given by the Spirit of God to man (Luke 22:31-32; John 17:11). It means such imparted life is necessarily permanent, indestructible so that the once regenerate and believing man has the prospect of final glory infallibly assured. *Who shall lay any thing to the charge of God's elect? It is God that justifieth. Who is he that condemneth? It is Christ that died, yea rather, that is risen again, who is even at the right hand of God, who also maketh intercession for us. Who shall separate us from the love of Christ? shall tribulation, or distress, or persecution, or famine, or nakedness, or peril, or sword? As it is written, For thy sake we are killed all the day long; we are accounted as sheep for the slaughter. Nay, in all these things we are more than conquerors through him that loved us. For I am persuaded, that neither death, nor life, nor angels, nor principalities, nor powers, nor things present, nor things to come, Nor height, nor depth, nor any other creature, shall be able to separate us from the love of God, which is in Christ Jesus our Lord.*—Romans 8:33-39.

Scripture on the one hand abounds with assurances of 'preservation' as a fact, and largely intimates that an exulting anticipation of it is the intended experience of the believer. *And I give unto them eternal life; and they shall never perish, neither shall any man pluck them out of my hand.*—John 10:28 (compare Romans 8:31-37; 1Peter 1:8-9).

At the same time, it laid down 'preservation' as the divine rule for the Christian, while the negative passages set to caution the man not to deceive himself with appearances, nor to let any belief whatever palliate the guilt and minimize the danger of sin. *If ye continue in the faith grounded and settled, and be not moved away from the hope of the gospel, which ye have heard, and which was preached to every creature which is under heaven; whereof I Paul am made a minister;*—Colossians 1:23; (John 8:31; Hebrews 3:6, 14).

## Predestination

Predestination is fundamentally important in that it reaches down to the Infinite Will of God in relation to the universe of finite wills, and lays stress on will as the core of reality. It is that aspect of foreordination whereby the salvation of the believer is brought to pass in accordance with the will of God, who has called and elected him, in Christ, unto life eternal. *Moreover whom he did predestinate, them he also called: and whom he called, them he also justified: and whom he justified, them he also glorified.*—Romans 8:30; (Ephesians 1:4, 5, 9).

## Resurrection

Paul in addressing his defence at the first trial at Felix's court spoke of the doctrine of resurrection. *And have hope toward God, which they themselves also allow, that there shall be a resurrection of the dead, both of the just and unjust.*—Acts 24:15. Jesus refers to it in John 5:28,29: *Marvel not at this: for the hour is coming, in the which all that are in the graves shall hear his voice, And shall come forth; they that have done good, unto the resurrection of life; and they that have done evil, unto the resurrection of damnation.* There are clearly two resurrections: the resurrection of life, and the resurrection of damnation or judgement. Further reviews of John 6:50, 8:51; 11:24-44, teach that the resurrection of life refers to *present* eternal life possessed by those who believe in Christ as their personal Saviour. Resurrection of the dead is *future.* (*Verily, verily, I say unto you, He that believeth on me hath everlasting life. I am that bread of life. Your fathers did eat manna in the wilderness, and are dead. This is the bread which cometh down from heaven, that a man may eat thereof, and not die*)

# 10

---

# Where am I heading?

*For thou art my lamp, O LORD:*
*and the LORD will lighten my darkness.*
—2 Samuel 22: 29

What I mean by having this chapter titled in a question "Where am I heading?" is that in the Christian Gospel that conflict of duties confines itself not only to the man; it reflects itself in its full intensity in the life of the eternal God. That God is righteous and infinitely holy, we reverently believe. That God is merciful and infinitely loving, we learn from the teachings we receive. The whole New Testament is but the story of infinite wisdom of God, reconciling in a way most wonderful—*His infinite righteousness and boundless love.* I was, as a young Christian, a part for fitting into Christ's church—a 'building' that had for its foundation Christ's redemptive work: he was made a ransom for God's consuming wrath set on wayward man. In His resurrection, His redemptive work accomplished, God the Father gave us a comforter in the Holy Spirit He who lives or breathes in us of Himself, His very nature, His character to continue the building through the ages until its completion, when Christ comes again as King to receive His Kingdom. My heart and mind—trained and focused on what it took to be a Christian, the works to undertake to be one—failed to see Christ's ultimate work. I was looking at my own man in my work to meet Christ and missed the greater work of Christ. *For the Son of man is as a man taking a far journey, who left his house, and gave authority to his servants, and to every man his work, and commanded the porter to watch. Watch ye therefore: for ye know not when the master of the house cometh, at even, or at midnight, or at the cockcrowing, or in the morning: Lest coming suddenly he find you sleeping. And what I say unto you I say unto all, Watch.*—Mark 13:4-37

In reflection now as I write, I am finally clear of my purpose: that, as Christ became God-man in obedience (self-denial) to God the Father, walked upon the face of this world, went through the cross (self-sacrifice) and into glory; we individually must follow Christ, bear our cross, and traverse this early journey till we enter into His glory. Now that we are clear where we are heading, we can with patience in the all sufficiency of His grace, follow Him in faith. Cast aside the thought of burdens that beset us, the weight that drags us down, the slippery ground that imperil our every step, the oft times hopelessness that beckons us to give in and give up. Count on Christ for all His promises, count on His strength, His wisdom, His love, His mercy, and goodness. Trials and afflictions are our portion in life, can we put them aside? Can we pass it off to another?

*Beloved, think it not strange concerning the fiery trial which is to try you, as though some strange thing happened unto you: But rejoice, inasmuch as ye are partakers of Christ's sufferings; that, when his glory shall be revealed, ye may be glad also with exceeding joy. If ye be reproached for the name of Christ, happy are ye; for the spirit of glory and of God resteth upon you: on their part he is evil spoken of, but on your part he is glorified.*—1 Peter 4:12-14. *Yet man is born unto trouble, as the sparks fly upward.*—Job 5:7. *Man that is born of a woman is of few days, and full of trouble. He cometh forth like a flower, and is cut down: he fleeth also as a shadow, and continueth not.*—Job 14:1-2. *These things I have spoken unto you, that in me ye might have peace. In the world ye shall have tribulation: but be of good cheer; I have overcome the world.*—John 16:33.

*God is our refuge and strength, a very present help in trouble. Therefore will not we fear, though the earth be removed, and though the mountains be carried into the midst of the sea; Though the waters thereof roar and be troubled, though the mountains shake with the swelling thereof.*—Psalm 46:1-3.

*God shall hear, and afflict them, even he that abideth of old. Selah. Because they have no changes, therefore they fear not God.*—Psalm 55:19.

*And let us not be weary in well doing: for in due season we shall reap, if we faint not. As we have therefore opportunity, let us do good unto all men, especially unto them who are of the household of faith.*—Galatians 6:9-10.

To what will I give my life? Is it going to be to a career? Is it going to be to pleasure and entertainment? Is it going to be to amassing wealth? Or is it going to be to God's purpose? Is it to the church I go to worship with other Christians?

I gave my life to follow Christ in so much as Christ gave me the Life in Him, the earthly life He lived, trod, and suffered, that I might have the new life, that I might have life everlasting.

That purpose appeared relegated to backstage, crowded out by the environment at church without first settling the matter with Scripture. Running from one activity to another as though works was central to Christianity, drew me away from grace. Expressing a 'feel-good' attitude all around, disregarded the true state of self and others. Uttering canned Scripture verses without seriously considering their contextual meaning and intention, misconstrued the Truth. Soul winning meant taking someone to church or to rallies, where 'winning' was more important than the soul. All of the above appeared to call attention to the 'self' and not to Christ. Fellowship with other Christians tend to set one in conformity with them and I found it very difficult, very vexing, for to question was as an indication of being at odds with the church. I was a babe in Christ and still learning; I needed to read for myself, to discover, and to understand all that Scripture has in store for the willing heart. I needed time away from the 'madding crowd', from the Christian activity that simply whisked one away from considering God's Word with much intensity. Counsel was generally canned. *But it is good for me to draw near to God: I have put my trust in the Lord GOD, that I may declare all thy works.*—Psalm 73:28. I needed time and space to re-think all that have passed rather quickly in five years. So, God helped me.

# 11

## WHAT IS THE WAY?

*And whither I go ye know, and the way ye know. Thomas saith
unto him, Lord, we know not whither thou goest; and how can
we know the way?
Jesus saith unto him, I am the way, the truth, and the life: no
man cometh unto the Father, but by me.*
—John 14:5-6

*I am the LORD thy God, which brought thee out of the land of
Egypt: open thy mouth wide, and I will fill it.*
—Psalm 81:10.

The Strong's definition of 'way' is *apparently a primary word; a road;
by implication a progress (the route, act or distance); figuratively a
mode or means:—journey, (high-) way.* By a simple and natural
figure 'way' is applied to the course of human conduct, the manner of life
which one lives. Yet almost invariably, Scripture accounts on the one hand
attached an ethical estimation to the way of human nature for good or
evil; on the other, God directed and ordered them in His perfect nature as
infinite, eternal, and immaculate. God's purposes and plans point toward
man's salvation; they and His provisions in as much are centred in Christ,
Christ is pre-eminently the Way to God. The Way to God is the Way to
heaven. 'All roads lead to Rome', so goes the saying, but truly no other way

will lead you to heaven, save the Way, save Christ Jesus, the only begotten son of God.

There is no access to the Father but by Christ. It is unto the Father that Christ is the Way: *no man cometh unto the Father, but by me.* Christ is the Way by being the Truth and the Life. It is as in 'I am the Truth and the Life because I am the Way'. Have faith in Him, the Way, and you will know and see the Truth. In the Truth you will find your life in Christ, the true Life. Get on the Way in faith, He will show you the Truth about Him, and about you. There on the Way, you will find your eternal life in following His Life. The Way is primary; the Truth and the Life are as explanatory to the Way. In a sense, *I am the Way because I am the Truth and the Life.*

Thomas' question "*how do we know the way?*" begs of ignorance yet there have been many occasions Christ had expressed His imminent death and His resurrection. The absolute answer from Jesus was that famous line. In proclaiming Himself 'the Way', Christ pronounces Himself the only One able to bridge and consummate the union between God-and-man and conditions as separate as heaven and earth, sin and holiness, the poor creature I know myself to be and the infinite and eternal God who is so righteous I cannot know Him. Christ restores that broken relationship.

> "I am the way, the truth, and the life. Without the way, there is no going; without the truth there is no knowing; without the life there is no living. I am the way which thou should pursue; the truth which thou should believe; the life which thou should hope for."—Thomas a Kempis, *Imitation of Christ*

The highway is ever so broad and straight, open to all, with few or no obstruction; it is an easy way to get on so as to get to the destination quickly. The Way of Christ is narrow, constricted, undulating, weaving about many obstacles, unseen dangers, discouragingly desolate, heinous at times, beset with difficulties. The Way progresses us to the Truth and to the Life.

> "These are the stages of the inner Way, which the saints have trodden before us: Detachment from the ambitions, passions, and sins of nature; Attachment, i.e., the attitude of fellowship

with Christ; Illumination, which reveals to the soul its unworthiness; Union with God. This is the experience of few, but they who have described it remind us that eye hath not seen, nor ear heard, what God's Spirit reveals to those who love and wait for Him. But you must be prepared to sacrifice all. He, who seeks diamonds, or gold, will face hardships and relinquish much that other men hold dear, that he may prosecute his quest. Not otherwise must it be with those who would understand the fear of the Lord and find the knowledge of God."

—F. B. Meyer

# 12

## WHAT IS THE TRUTH?

*Pilate therefore said unto him, Art thou a king then? Jesus
answered, Thou sayest that I am a king. To this end was I born,
and for this cause came I into the world, that I should bear witness
unto the truth. Every one that is of the truth heareth my voice.
Pilate saith unto him, What is truth? And when he had said
this, he went out again unto the Jews, and saith unto them, I
find in him no fault at all.*
—John 18:37-38.

In the above questioning by Pilate about Jesus' Jewish kingship, Jesus'
answer was in the affirmative and that He came to testify of the truth.
Those who hears His voice, not just the sound of it, but also having
an understanding thereof, thereby moved to act with it. Pilate seemed keen
to get on with the business at hand and by his comment, he thought not
of it as question, that Jesus' response about truth was pointless as in all
ages past truth had been unsearchable with no end to knowing it. Why
then speak of truth? *Truth is about the true knowledge of God. It is the very
things that concern the life, the death and the resurrection of Christ. Truth is
changeless; time does not reconstruct Truth; advances in science and profusion
of new ages do not moderate Truth.*

"The truth frequently seems unreasonable. The truth frequently is depressing. The truth sometimes seems to be evil. But it has the eternal advantage. It is the truth and what is built thereon neither brings nor yields confusion."—*Henry Ford.*

"Some men practically fall over truth, but pick themselves up and go on as if nothing happened."—*Winston Churchill.*

Ford may not have Eternal Truth in mind when he uttered those words yet there is earthly *truth* enough for us to think about. At least he tried to recognise truth for what he thought it was—that truth . . . does not cause confusion. That was also classic Churchill telling us the *truth* about the truth—that we all have problem grappling with truth. Truth for these two luminaries in industry and in politics were very likely the truth out of human reasoning and observation, relative to their times. They may skirt about truth but never quite get to the centre of truth. There is truly an absolute truth that is unchanging. The search for, and recognition of truth has been with man in a long time. The author himself had been looking for truth about two decades of his early life, it had initially seemed like a done deal, and as the years wore on, that truth wore off as well. He was certain it was not the truth. He found Truth only when he met Jesus the Christ; he was *ever learning, and never able to come to the knowledge of the truth.*—2 Timothy 3:7. Man will never know truth from any source other than Christ for He is the way, the truth, and the life.

When one has walked some distance in the divine Way, he begins to desire a fuller understanding of the reasons of the Way. Then Christ comes as the Truth, disclosing the grounds on which religious duty rests, satisfying thus the speculative faculty, as He did the practical.

I am the Truth. Were these words merely equivalent to "I speak the truth," it would be far much to know this of the One who tells us things of so measureless a consequence to ourselves; the faith of the disciples strained by what He had just been saying to them. Here was a man in most respects like themselves: a man who got hungry and sleepy, a man who was to be arrested and executed by the rulers, assuring them that He was going to prepare for them everlasting habitations, and that He would return to take them to these 'mansions' in His Father's house. He saw that they found it hard to believe this. Who does not find it hard to believe all our Lord tells us of our future? Think how much we trust simply to His word. If He is not true, then the whole of Christendom has framed its life on a false belief, and met at death by blank disappointment. Christ has aroused in our minds by His promises and statements, a group of ideas and expectations that nothing but His word could have persuaded us to entertain. Nothing is more remarkable about our Lord than the calmness and assurance with which He utters the most astounding statements. The most able and most enlightened men have their hesitations, their periods of agonising doubt, their suspense of judgment, their laboured inquiries, their mental conflicts. With Jesus, we can find none of this. From first to last He sees with perfect clearness to the utmost bound of human thought, knows with absolute certainty whatever is essential for us to know. His is not the assurance of ignorance, nor is it the dogmatic approach of a traditional teacher, nor the evasive assurance of a superficial and reckless mind. It is plainly the assurance of one who stands in the full noon of truth and speaks what He knows.

In His endeavours to gain the confidence of men, there is no discernible anger at their incredulity. Again and again, He brings forward reasons why His word should be believed. He appeals to their knowledge of His candour: "If it were not so, I would have told you." It was the *Truth* He came into the world for to bear witness; witness amidst the lies of man. He came to be the Light of the world, to dispel the darkness and bring men into the very truth of things. But with all His impressiveness in emphatic assertion there is no anger, scarcely even wonder that men did not believe, because He saw as plainly as we see that to venture our eternal hope on His word is not easy. And yet He answered promptly and with authority the questions that have employed the lifetime of many and baffled them in the end. He answered them as if they were the very alphabet of knowledge. These alarmed and perturbed disciples ask Him: "Is there a life beyond? Is there another side of death?" "Yes," He says, "through death I go to the Father." "Is there," they ask, "for us also a life beyond? Shall such creatures as we find sufficient and suitable habitation and welcome when we pass from this warm, well-known world?" "In My Father's house," He says, "are many mansions." Confronted with the problems that most deeply exercise the human spirit, He without faltering pronounces upon them. For every question that our most anxious and trying experiences dictate, He has the ready and sufficient answer. "He is the Truth."

But more than this is contained in His words. He says not merely, "I speak the truth," but "I am the Truth." In His person and work, we find all truth that it is essential to know. He is the true Man, the revelation of perfect manhood, in whom we see what human life truly is. In His own history, He shows us our own capacities and our own destiny. An inanimate law might *tell* us the truth about human life, but Christ is the Truth, not about the truth. He is man like us. If we, at death expire and are forever extinguished, so is He. If for us there is no future life, neither is there for Him. He is Himself human like us or we like Him.

Further and especially, He is the truth about God: "If ye had known me, ye had known My Father also." Strenuous efforts are made in our day to convince us that our search after God is vain, because by the very nature of the case it is impossible to know God. We are assured that all our imaginations of God are but a reflection of ourselves magnified infinitely; and that what results from all our thinking is not God, but only a magnified man. We form and hold in our thoughts an ideal of human excellence: perfect holiness and perfect love; and we add to this highest moral character we can conceive a supernatural power and wisdom, and this we call God. But this, we are assured, is but to mislead ourselves. Whatever we set before our minds as Divine is not God, but only a higher kind or order of man, imagined in our limited human faculties. But God is not a higher kind of man: He is a different kind of being, a Being to whom it is absurd to ascribe intelligence, or will, or personality, or anything human; He is omniscient. He knows all and sees all.

We have felt the force of what is thus urged; and feeling most deeply that for us the greatest of all questions is, 'What is God'? How can we even dare to ask the question? We have been afraid lest we delude ourselves with an image of our own concoction very different from the reality. We have felt that there is a great truth lying at the heart of the question or thought— the truth that we cannot find out God, cannot comprehend Him. We say certain things about Him, as that He is a Spirit; but which of us knows what a pure spirit is, which of us can conceive in our minds a distinct idea of what we so freely speak of as a spirit? Indeed, it is because it is impossible for us to have any sufficient idea of God, as He is in Himself that He has become man and manifested Himself in flesh.

This revelation of God in man implies that there is an affinity and likeness between God and man, that man is made in God's image. Were it not so, we should see in Christ, not God at all, but only man. If God is manifest in Christ, it is because there is that in God which can find suitable expression in a human life and person. In fact, this revelation takes for granted that in a sense it is quite true that God is a magnified Man, that He is a Being in whom there is much that resembles what is in man. And it stands to reason that this must be so. It is quite true that man can only conceive what is like himself; but that is only half the truth. It is also true that God can only create what is consistent with His own mind. In His creatures, we see a reflection of Himself. And as we ascend from the lowest of them to the highest, we see what He considers the highest qualities. Finding in ourselves these highest qualities, qualities that enable us to understand all lower creatures and to use them, we gather that in God Himself there must be something akin to our mind and to our inner man.

Christ, then, is 'the Truth', because He reveals God. In Him, we learn what God is and how to approach Him. But knowledge is not enough. It is conceivable that we should have learned much about God and yet have despaired of ever becoming like Him. It might gradually have become our conviction that we were for ever shut out from all good, although that is incompatible with a true knowledge of God; for if God is known at all, He must be known as Love, as self-communicating. But the possibility of having knowledge that we cannot use is precluded by the fact that He who is the Truth is also the Life. In Him who reveals we at the same time find power to avail ourselves of the revelation.

*Howbeit when he, the Spirit of truth, is come, he will guide you into all truth: for he shall not speak of himself; but whatsoever he shall hear, that shall he speak: and he will shew you things to come.—John 16:13.*

> "Truth is like a vast cavern into which we desire to enter, but we are not able to traverse it alone. At the entrance, it is clear and bright; but if we would go further and explore its innermost recesses, we must have a guide, or we shall lose ourselves. The

Holy Spirit, who knows all truth perfectly, is the appointed guide of all true believers, and He conducts them as they are able to bear it, from one inner chamber to another, so that they behold the deep things of God, and His secret is made plain to them. What a promise is this for the humbly inquiring mind! We desire to know the truth and to enter into it. We are conscious of our own aptness to err, and we feel the urgent need of a guide. We rejoice that the Holy Spirit is come and abides among us. He condescends to act as a guide to us, and we gladly accept His leadership. 'All truth' we wish to learn that we may not be one-sided and out of balance. We would not be willingly ignorant of any part of revelation lest thereby we should miss blessing or incur sin. The Spirit of God has come that He may guide us into all truth: let us with obedient hearts hearken to His words and follow His lead." —*C.H. Spurgeon.*

Truth is reality in relation to the vital interests of the soul. It is primarily to be realized and done, rather than to be learned or known. Truth is in part apprehended, and in part to be borne of. The will to bear truth, to do God's will, is the requisite manner to apprehend the truth. It is in doing His will that we can experience and therefore truly understand the truth. *If any man will do his will, he shall know of the doctrine, whether it be of God, or whether I speak of myself. He that speaketh of himself seeketh his own glory: but he that seeketh his glory that sent him, the same is true, and no unrighteousness is in him.*—John 7:17-18. What is the truth? *Then said Jesus to those Jews which believed on him, If ye continue in my word, then are ye my disciples indeed; And ye shall know the truth, and the truth shall make you free.*—John 8:31-32.

In apprehending the truth, we must do God's will, that which is found in Scripture, requiring us to 'rightly divide' the Word (2 Timothy 2:15). What is discernment of the truth? 'Discern' in Scripture is very often to differentiate extremes as in *the noise of the shout of joy from the noise of the weeping* (Ezra 3:13); *the difference between the holy and profane, and cause them to discern between the unclean and the clean* (Ezekiel 44:23); *between their right hand and their left hand* (Jonah 4:11); *between the righteous and the wicked, between him that serveth God and him that serveth him not* (Malachi 3:18); *discern both good and evil* (Hebrews 5:14). There must be a standard by which we can divide and discern. In the Scripture, the known will of God is final as a standard of truth, not as arbitrary, but as expressive of God's nature. God's nature is all-comprehensive of fact and goodness, and so is, all and in all, the source, support and objective of all concrete being. The will of God thus reveals, persuades to and achieves the ideals and ends of complete existence. The term 'truth' is sometimes, therefore, nearly equivalent to the revealed will of God. *Sanctify them through thy truth: thy word is truth.*—John 17:17.

In a sense, the gospel is the truth. *In whom ye also trusted, after that ye heard the word of truth, the gospel of your salvation.*—Ephesians 1:13.

Truth is personalized in Jesus Christ. He truly is an expression of God, presents the true ideal of man, in Himself summarizes the harmony of existence and becomes the agent to unify and reconcile the disordered world to God. Hence, He is the Truth (John 14:6), the true expression '*logos*', (John 1:1) of God. See the same idea without the terminology in Paul. *In whom we have redemption through his blood, even the forgiveness of sins*—Colossians 1:14; *for in him dwelleth all the fulness of the Godhead bodily.*—Colossians 2:9. Similarly, the Holy Spirit is the Spirit of truth because His function is to guide into all truth. *Howbeit when he, the Spirit of truth, is come, he will guide you into all truth: for he shall not speak of himself; but whatsoever he shall hear, that shall he speak: and he will shew you things to come.*—John 16:13; *But the anointing which ye have received of him abideth in you, and ye need not that any man teach you: but as the same anointing teacheth you of all things, and is truth, and is no lie, and even as it hath taught you, ye shall abide in him.*—1 John 2:27. *For there are three that bear record in heaven, the Father, the Word, and the Holy Ghost: and these three are one.*—1 John 5:7

# 13

## WHAT IS THE LIFE?

*Jesus saith unto him, I am the way, the truth, and the life: no
man cometh unto the Father, but by me.*
—John 14:6

*Thou wilt shew me the path of life: in thy presence is fulness of
joy; at thy right hand there are pleasures for evermore.*
—Psalm 16:11.

Finally, Christ reveals Himself as the Life. Seen here, Christianity
is more than practice and knowledge, it is the communication of
vital powers, of the powers of the life of God, of power to become
the child of God; and that this new vitality in turn prompts to committed
pious practice, and facilitates spiritual perception.

The provisions of grace for our Christian life and work are boundless,
because *"God is able to make all grace abound to you, so that in all things at
all times, having all that you need, you will abound in every good work"*—2
Corinthians 9:8. The epistle to the church at Ephesus sums up this fact
of abundance, *now to him who is able to do immeasurably more than all we
ask or imagine, according to his power that is at work within us, to him be
glory in the church and in Christ Jesus throughout all generations, forever and
ever! Amen.*—Ephesians 3:20-21. We are therefore called upon to meet

God's high measure of redeeming grace by corresponding fullness in our Christian walk. *Rooted and built up in him, stablished in the faith as you were taught, with thanksgiving* (Colossians 2:7).

We are to abound in love. *"And this I pray, that your love may abound yet more and more in knowledge and in all judgment"*—Philippians 1:9. *"And the Lord make you to increase and abound in love one toward another, and toward all men, even as we do toward you"*—1 Thessalonians 3:12.

We are to abound in holiness. *"Finally brothers, we instructed you how to live in order to please God, as in fact you are living. Now we ask you and urge you in the Lord Jesus to do this more and more"*—1 Thessalonians 4:1.

We are to abound in joy. *"That your rejoicing may be more abundant in Jesus Christ for me by my coming to you again."*—Philippians 1:26.

We are to abound in hope. *"Now the God of hope fill you with all joy and peace in believing, that ye may abound in hope, through the power of the Holy Ghost."*—Romans 15:13. We are to abound in liberality, even to the depths of poverty. *"How that in a great trial of affliction the abundance of their joy and their deep poverty abounded unto the riches of their liberality."*—2 Corinthians 8:2-7.

"I am come that they might have life, and that they might have *it* more abundantly." (John 10:10). *Jesus said unto her, I am the resurrection, and the life: he that believeth in me, though he were dead, yet shall he live.*—John 11:25. *For in him we live, and move, and have our being; as certain also of your own poets have said, for we are also his offspring.*—Acts 17:28.

It is Jesus Christ who brings us into connection with this source of life eternal—He bears it in His own person. In Him, we receive a new spirit; in Him, our motive to live for righteousness continually revived, renewed; we become conscious that in Him we touch what is undying and that never fails to renew spiritual life in us. Whatever we need to give us true and everlasting life, we have in Christ. Whatever we need to enable us to come to the Father, whatever we shall need between this present stage of experience and our final stage, we have in Him, in His name.

The more, then, we apply to Christ and use Him, the more life we have. The more we are with Him and the more we partake of His Spirit, the fuller will our own life become. It is not by imitating successful and famous men that we become influential for good, but by living with Christ. It is not by adopting the habits and methods of saints that we become strong and useful, but by accepting Christ and His Spirit. Nothing can take the place of Christ. Nothing can take His words and say to us, "I am the Life." We desire the Life, yet see that we are doing little good, and desire energy to overtake what needs to be done, it is to Him we must go. When we feel all our efforts were vain, that they came to nought, that we no longer can bear up against our circumstances or against our own wicked nature; we can assuredly receive fresh fervour and hopefulness only from Christ. Let us not be downcast at our failures if we seem not to receive from Christ the life that is in Him. Nothing can give us the life that is in Him but our own personal application to Him, our direct dealing with Him as we partake of that highest of all forms of life—the life that is in Him, the living One, by whom all things were made, and who in the very face of death can say, "Because I live ye shall live also." *Verily, verily, I say unto you, He that believeth on me hath everlasting life.*—John 6:47. *And if Christ be in you, the body is dead because of sin; but the Spirit is life because of righteousness.*—Romans 8:10. *That which was from the beginning, which we have heard, which we have seen with our eyes, which we have looked upon, and our hands have handled, of the Word of life.*—1 John1:1. *For the wages of sin is death; but the gift of God is eternal life through Jesus Christ our Lord.*—Romans 6:23.

From Christ we draw His nature, His Person, and from Him we shall have His vitality, the very essence of the Life. Our life is in Him, so why find our own life? Why love thou thine own life when in losing it we shall have His Life? Let us with all vehemence seek to live the life of Christ. *He that findeth his life shall lose it: and he that loseth his life for my sake shall find it. He that receiveth you receiveth me, and he that receiveth me receiveth him that sent me.*—Matthew 10:38-39

# 14

## COME ye yourselves Apart . . . and Rest awhile

*And he said unto them, Come ye yourselves apart into a desert place, and rest a while: for there were many coming and going, and they had no leisure so much as to eat.*
—Mark 6:31

In the preceding verse 30, *and the apostles gathered themselves together unto Jesus, and told him all things, both what they had done, and what they had taught*, the apostles, now first called by that name, because these first 'that were sent' had carried the message of their Lord, returned and told Him all—the miracles they had wrought, and whatever they had taught. When Christ sent them out to preach 'that men should repent', they had to face derision, get into arguments, embroiled in motives, promises, perhaps threats, and manhandling, which rendered it no meagre pronouncement of the gospel. It is in truth a demand that involves free will and responsibility as its bases, and has hell or heaven for the result of disobedience or compliance. What controversies these first preachers of Jesus entered into they now submitted to the judgment of their Master. And happy are they still who do not shrink from the healing pain of bringing all their actions and words to Him, and to hearken what the Lord will speak.

On the whole, they brought accounts of success. And around Him also were so many coming and going that they had no leisure so much as to eat; whereupon Jesus draws them aside to rest awhile. For the balance must ever be wrought between the outer and the inner life. In the midst of a busy life on the outside, of doing and serving, we must often return to the rest in the inner, to fellowship with our Lord. We need to come apart and rest, to refresh and draw strength from the fountain of living water, from the Master Himself. *And they went away in the boat* privately *to a desert place apart. And the people saw them going, and many knew them, and they ran there together on foot from all the cities, and outwent them. And He came forth and saw a great multitude, and He had compassion on them, because they were as sheep not having a shepherd: and He began to teach them many things* (Mark 6:32-34).

On another occasion when Jesus after His resurrection appeared before His disciples, the small party of men who was now leaderless: He reveals His tender loving touch in a moment of loss. Desertion and drudgery; purpose lost; Saviour gone missing somewhere; mission grounded. There was a sense of emptiness, of forlorn hope, a brooding after loneliness; the vision of Christ lost. Peter decided to do what he had always done—fishing—an occupation he was as familiar with as breathing was as second nature. *Simon Peter saith unto them, I go a fishing. They say unto him, we also go with thee. They went forth, and entered into a ship immediately; and that night they caught nothing.*—John 21:3. Their Saviour stood out and drew near. They knew Him not. He knows of our spoils, He feels our broken spirits, He ever longs to comfort, to hold us up when all else seems forlorn and lost. *After these things Jesus shewed himself again to the disciples at the sea of Tiberias; and on this wise shewed he himself. But when the morning was now come, Jesus stood on the shore: but the disciples knew not that it was Jesus. Then Jesus saith unto them, Children, have ye any meat? They answered him, No. And he said unto them, Cast the net on the right side of the ship, and ye shall find. They cast therefore, and now they were not able to draw it for the multitude of fishes. Therefore that disciple whom Jesus loved saith unto Peter, It is the Lord. Now when Simon Peter heard that it was the Lord, he girt his fisher's coat unto him, (for he was naked,) and did cast himself into the sea.*—John 21:4-7.

The Lord had been most gracious and merciful when He called us apart to rest, so that the season of trial does not become a season of temptation. When all else seemed lost, perhaps uncertain, hope floating listlessly as though the natural law of gravity momentarily suspended, the laws of nature for a space in time came to a halt; there was nothing one could do but drift into an attitude of 'live, and let live'; neither stoic nor fatalistic nor a feeling of abandonment. Such times were dangerous times, they stood at the edge of the abyss of temptation, they stood at the door to darkness, and they opened up to the broad way of deceiving hope. The devil was there to tell you that you have made a mistake in following Christ. That you would be the wiser to set your eyes on your career, time to accumulate wealth, the churches were all a sham, the church Christians were fake, merely professors of their faith; that there is no heaven while you experience hell on earth. That you turn away from Christ; for, the worst in your life had manifested when you followed Christ. Why should you be vexed and suffer when you can make a break and do it your own way. That the Bible and Christ have deceived you; the devil continues to cast aspersions in your way.

> *O Father let us with patience run,*
> *Let Thy judgement be as the noonday sun.*
> *Teach us never from Christ to stray,*
> *For He saith, 'I am the Way'.*
>
> *O Father, let us with wisdom pray,*
> *In Thy will may all our hopes lay.*
> *Counsel us to walk and honour Thee:*
> *'I am the Truth', for so proclaim He.*
>
> *O Father, let us with earnest seek,*
> *In all Thy endeavours, may we be meek.*
> *Strengthen us to glorify Thee with all might,*
> *'I am the Life', for in Him is our Light.*

How often has He given me 'time off' by His act of watchful love and providential care? He sends it when my need was deeply hurtful and sore, my burden grudgingly weighted and heavy. It was always 'in time', never a moment too early or too late, up to the last fraying strand in the rope of life, when all the walls closed in and the light shut out; yet affording a single last breath before His hand reaches out to lift me from that fearful rut. It was as a time when the hen called for her chicks to come under her *brooding* wings, the wings they trusted and where they were safe. *The LORD recompense thy work, and a full reward be given thee of the LORD God of Israel, under whose wings thou art come to trust.*—Ruth 2:12

The author, newly born five years earlier, was caught up in activities every fervent believer wanted to do when they followed Christ. All that kept a wide space between him and Christ. He missed the true deep fellowship with God. Now, he needed solitude away from the worldly din, to meditate on those gracious things which God has done for him. That it may frame a larger, deeper, more adequate conception of what salvation really is. That his gratitude may become more precise and more profound; that, with nothing and no one to distract, he may dedicate itself quietly and fully to His Lord. The Apostle Paul after his conversion did not immediately go out to preach; only three years did he go up to Jerusalem, *"neither went I up to Jerusalem to them which were apostles before me; but I went into Arabia, and returned again unto Damascus. Then after three years I went up to Jerusalem to see Peter, and abode with him fifteen days."*—Galatians 1:17-18

# 15

## Out of the WOODS;
## Still in the WILDERNESS

*For, lo, he that formeth the mountains, and createth the wind,
and declareth unto man what is his thought, that maketh the
morning darkness, and treadeth upon the high places of the
earth, The LORD, The God of hosts, is his name.*
—Amos 4:13.

We entered into the narrow *way* of God when we acknowledged *truth* as of Christ in that we received spiritual sight in God's light where, for once, we stepped out of darkness into the *life* led by the Spirit of God and exemplified in Christ. We shall expect to walk this earthly sojourn with every decision we make as we carry our daily crosses and traverse the valleys and arrive at our Christian triumphs; they will occur and recur to strengthen and refine us until we enter into His glory. The earth is our wilderness, and in that wilderness are many woods, some more dense than others. We may see beyond the trees to the woods, yet coming out of one only to enter another. As long as we are in the wilderness, we may encounter more woods. In the age of brooding, we truly enter a maturing process. In the *wilderness of brooding*, we learnt lessons of humility in the beauty He surrounds us with; in the wilderness of brooding we struggle through hunger and thirst for perfect peace with God; in the wilderness of brooding we discover the dangers of working for the Lord in our own perception (and will) instead of working in the Lord's will. We have yet to learn of submission to His will. Very often, we miss the call to faith in Christ. *For by grace are ye saved through faith; and that not of yourselves: it is the gift of God: not of works, lest any man should boast.*—Ephesians 2:8-9.

God never blesses non-purposed and unplanned labour. That is the labour of the thirteenth hour. All that God calls us to, and all that love demands, He framed us fitly with perfect wisdom to the twelve hours before it. In Him we trust, we can be restful and not be in disquietude; we do not fret and fidget; He will afford us a little leisure for smiling and for sleep. There is no time to waste away and squander, but with the Lord, there is always time enough—are there not twelve hours in the day? All that passed not wasted; all to come not squandered if only we would trust and obey. God directs and leads His people in the wilderness; He lets loose His grip as He sees fit, He restrains and constrains as He wills, He holds up and lowers according to our strength or weakness. In all that He causes, He lovingly sustains. *Who led thee through that great and terrible wilderness, wherein were fiery serpents, and scorpions, and drought, where there was no water; who brought thee forth water out of the rock of flint; who fed thee in the wilderness with manna, which thy fathers knew not, that he might humble thee, and that he might prove thee, to do thee good at thy latter end.*—Deuteronomy 8:15-16.

> "God takes the most eminent and choicest of His servants for the choicest and most eminent afflictions. They who have received most grace from God are able to bear most afflictions from God. Affliction does not hit the saint by chance, but by direction. God does not draw His bow at a venture. Every one of His arrows goes upon a special errand and touches no breast but his against whom it is sent. It is not only the grace, but the glory of a believer when we can stand and take affliction quietly."—*Joseph Caryl*

Wait not for the thirteenth hour. We are nearing the end of the twelfth. Have faith in the saving grace of our Lord Jesus Christ. Come to Him now. Tarry no more. *As many as I love, I rebuke and chasten: be zealous therefore, and repent.*—Revelation 3:19

# EPILOGUE

*Enough, enough, what Jesus says!*
*I'll boast infirmity!*
*In conflict, sorrow, darkness, death,*
*Your grace suffices me!*
—Newman Hall

L ife in its flow is like a music score. The bars in the music sets the time, the note in its value of time and its place on the staff define its pitch and length, enhanced by various accentuations, staccatos, legatos, rests, pauses, slurs, crescendos/decrescendos, volumes (*pianissimo* to *fortissimo*). Life goes through these shades, some scores with less, some more, others sad, contemplative, moody, and still others lively and vivacious.

Yet we see in Christ, in His simplicity that touches our want of simplicity in the midst of a constantly changing world, the music need not be overcrowding to include all the glamorous strains for a grand rendition. His music is as simple as the little brook chattering and gurgling among the pebbles, sparkling in the water's surface under the gentle sun, cooled by the light caressing breeze, and the lining of low trees bearing fruit in their due season. It is as the excited tugs on the heart strings as we sense His touch speaking in a noiseless low hum "I love thee." The peace of the Lord surpasses all understanding. He uses our sighs, our sniffs in tears, our discomforts, our pains, our moans, groans, and travails to bring forth the strains of love and comfort that He sends back to our hearts and lift us into songs of praise.

God our Heavenly Father, in His Infinite Wisdom is the Master Composer, Jesus the Immaculate Conductor interprets the score faithfully, and the Holy Spirit quickens us, the musicians, to manifest the praise, honour, and glory of our Almighty Creator.

Faith in Christ was absolutely fundamental to support all that I believe about Him as written in the gospels. That God the Father sent Him, God the Son, who was blameless and without sin, who in willing obedience to the Father, was born in the flesh and live as man in a sinful world, without the trappings of a divine prince. Faith was an undying trust in Christ even in the midst of severe loss and/or death.

Can we come to Him in faith then? We assuredly can. We must first come in faith, not weak faith. It must be a *humble faith* willing to cast all else aside just to follow Jesus: for He gave up all to be our redeemer. He is the Way, the Truth, and the Life. It is a faith that regards not who we are: our station, our past glories, our qualifications, our capabilities or incapability, our brilliance or ineptitude, our recognition in the world, our genius. This humble faith relies only upon Christ in all His promises. How can we rely on our own strength when there is none, but the blemishes of sin? We are weak against the wiles of the devil who knows our weak spots that lay in our flesh. Only Christ saves.

Next, as we go on the road, on the journey in life where raging unknowns buffet us, the challenges surprise us, the worldly demands work against us, the unbelieving world mocks at us, derides to shake our foundations. We must then draw on a *meek faith* that submits to God's will and not take things into our own hands, trusting Him for the provisions to take us through and thereby glorifying Him. We simply have no *rights* of our own except those that we have in our adoption in Christ. *But without faith it is impossible to please him: for he that cometh to God must believe that he is, and that he is a rewarder of them that diligently seek him.*—Hebrews 11:6.

Will this Epilogue lead to another Prologue? Why not, if He speaks so, His will commands so. Who knows save the Lord? *For my thoughts are not your thoughts, neither are your ways my ways, saith the LORD. For as the heavens are higher than the earth, so are my ways higher than your ways, and my thoughts than your thoughts.*—Isaiah 55:8-9. As long as we roam this earth, we look forward to another prologue, to another experience in the Lord, fully assured that we mature in going forth. The value of proofing is immense in developing faith in Christ, establishing us in stature before God and men.

As for me, the words I pray to hear of the Lord are: "Well done, thou good and faithful servant". For a servant I am to do His bidding and commands, to move as He wills, to act as He directs. I shall be content thus to be.

The Lord Jesus after calling us apart to rest never leaves us alone. He comes around to feed and fellowship with us, to remind us of His presence always. He bids us to come dine with Him. He breaks bread and more with fish, and serves us. *Jesus saith unto them, Come and dine. And none of the disciples durst ask him, Who art thou? knowing that it was the Lord. Jesus then cometh, and taketh bread, and giveth them, and fish likewise.*—John 21:2-3. Can we leave Him? We are touched at His perfect timing of fellowship when we are hopelessly broken for He had been ever watching over and caring for us. He bids us come and dine. *He breaks not the bruised reed.* His staff comforts us when our broken spirits sink low in the valley of the shadow of death. He walks with us and beside us, by His rod He holds us up, draws us close up, chastens, and strengthens us. He bids us come and dine. He takes us up to the mountaintops where we once again see the light and heaven in all its glories. *He quenches not the smoking flax.* Let us be faithful and set the Lord before us always. *I have set the LORD always before me: because he is at my right hand, I shall not be moved. Therefore my heart is glad, and my glory rejoiceth: my flesh also shall rest in hope.*—Psalm 16:8-9

*O LORD, thou hast searched me, and known me.*

*Thou knowest my downsitting and mine uprising, thou understandest my thought afar off.*

*Thou compassest my path and my lying down, and art acquainted with all my ways. For there is not a word in my tongue, but, lo, O LORD, thou knowest it altogether.*

*Thou hast beset me behind and before, and laid thine hand upon me. Such knowledge is too wonderful for me; it is high, I cannot attain unto it.*

*Whither shall I go from thy spirit?*

*Or whither shall I flee from thy presence?*

*If I ascend up into heaven, thou art there: if I make my bed in hell, behold, thou art there.*

*If I take the wings of the morning, and dwell in the uttermost parts of the sea; Even there shall thy hand lead me, and thy right hand shall hold me.*

*If I say, Surely the darkness shall cover me; even the night shall be light about me. Yea, the darkness hideth not from thee; but the night shineth as the day: the darkness and the light are both alike to thee.*

*For thou hast possessed my reins: thou hast covered me in my mother's womb.*

*I will praise thee; for I am fearfully and wonderfully made: marvellous are thy works; and that my soul knoweth right well. My substance was not hid from thee, when I was made in secret, and curiously wrought in the lowest parts of the earth. Thine eyes did see my substance, yet being unperfect; and in thy book all my members were written, which in continuance were fashioned, when as yet there was none of them.*

*How precious also are thy thoughts unto me, O God! How great is the sum of them!*

*If I should count them, they are more in number than the sand: when I awake, I am still with thee. Surely thou wilt slay the wicked, O God: depart from me therefore, ye bloody men. For they speak against thee wickedly, and thine enemies take thy name in vain. Do not I hate them, O LORD, that hate thee? And am not I grieved with those that rise up against thee? I hate them with perfect hatred: I count them mine enemies.*

*Search me, O God, and know my heart: try me, and know my thoughts: and see if there be any wicked way in me, and lead me in the way everlasting.—*
Psalm 139

"O Love that wilt not let me go,
I rest my weary soul in Thee,
I give Thee back the life I owe,
That in thine ocean depths its flow
May richer, fuller be.

"O Light that followest all my way,
I yield my flickering torch to Thee,
My heart restores its borrowed ray,
That in Thy sunshine's blaze its day
May brighter, fairer be.

"O Joy that seekest me through pain,
I cannot close my heart to Thee,
I trace the rainbow through the rain,
And feel the promise is not vain,
That morn shalt tearless be.

"O Cross that liftest up my head,
I dare not ask to fly from Thee,
I lay in dust life's glory dead,
And from the ground there blossoms red,
Life that shall endless be."

—George Matheson

# A ♩♩ to READERS

You may have read one or several of the earlier three books:

- Age of Innocence
- Age of Discovery
- Age of Restlessness

This book, **Age of Brooding** published in soft cover, hard cover, and e-book versions, is available from Trafford Publishing Singapore.

You can also avail of it online at Amazon, Barnes & Noble, Book Depository, Kinokuniya, and many others. You may visit my Facebook page and search for Robin P. Blessed. There are links to the online bookstores.

Rejoice with me! We have finally made it to the fourth and last book in the **Age of . . .** sequel. It has been an eye-opening and searching journey. What we had started out to accomplish, is now completed. Our lives are no different in that there are always beginnings and endings. The Lord informs us of our beginning and reveals to us our end. What we *willingly* take up, we can *joyfully* lay down when we arrive at our destination through faith and perseverance. Blessed be the name of the LORD!

# ACKNOWLEDGEMENTS

***M**y first and highest acknowledgement shall always be to God.* I find Andrew Bonar's expression most agreeable to my thought and feeling when he wrote, "My righteousness is the righteousness of Him who is God and our Saviour. I see nothing in myself but *that which* would condemn me to eternal banishment from God. I shall be to all eternity a debtor to the Lord my God, never paying one mite, but, on the contrary, hour by hour getting deeper and deeper and deeper in debt to Him who is 'all my salvation and all my desire.' I often exult in the thought that every moment in the ages to come I shall be better and better able to love Him Who loved me from all eternity—Who chose me—Who lived for me that life of obedience, and died that death in order that I, a soul that sinned, might live with Him forever. He rose, ascended, and interceded for me. He presented my name to the Father as one of the lost whom He had found. He is coming in glory soon to claim my body from the grave, and to make me altogether perfect, spotless, glorious, the image of Himself. I give all to the praise of the glory of His grace! All this is mine because He has enabled me to believe on the beloved Son. 'Accepted in the Beloved' shall be on my forehead along with the Father's name, in New Jerusalem. By grace, through faith: Bless the Lord, O my soul!"

***My immediate family,*** *my parents (deceased) and my siblings (of whom one is deceased)* who may or may not have known about my writing has been a hidden group of silent motivators. Even though 'silent', they have been an ineffaceable part of me as for a purpose; our lives permanently intertwined.

*The many brothers and sisters in* **my church family** *who truly have been supportive* of my writing endeavour are deserving of my humble thanks from the depths of my heart and soul: a big hearty and deeply grateful and warm embrace to them all. They kindly rendered to me a tenderly loving and kind pulse check of my writing.

*The many others in my life* who made a cameo appearance—named or anonymous—in this book or elsewhere in the earlier three books of the 'AGE OF . . .' sequel, as those had not been included in print for want of space and consistency. Life is never an accident and you were all fitted to His design.

*The publishing team at Trafford* and their consultants continued to be a blessing. Special mention with a vote of thanks accorded to Sydney Felicio who has an almost telepathic understanding in our communication, while she patiently worked with me through the four books in the *Age of* . . . sequel. Her patience and understanding have been a God-sent continuing exception.

# ABOUT THE AUTHOR

The author is semi-retired, a child of God by divine election, a financial services consultant and writer by calling, a coach by choice, a management consultant by circumstance and inclination, and an accountant by training. He is married with two adult children and two grandchildren, and lives in Singapore. He worships at a Bible-believing Baptist church. Robin writes under a pen name.

Robin believes that life is not accidental but has a purposeful design privy only to the Creator. He catches glimpses of it as he reflects on his own life. Time reveals a coherence of all of life's *past* events as he sees them dovetailed or integrated into the ultimate divine purpose.

This book *Age of Brooding* is the fourth and last of a planned sequel that seeks to understand a *concept* of life by reflecting on events and experiences occurring in their chronological stages of development, and revealing the completed part of the divine blueprint as he sees it. It offers insight into Robin's life between age 21 and 26, before he married and raised a family.

The first book was *Age of Innocence* published at the end of 2012. The second, *Age of Discovery* retailed in May 2013. The third book, *Age of Restlessness* became available in mid-September 2013.

All communications can reach the author at his personal email at blessedprobin@gmail.com or at his Facebook page (search for Robin P. Blessed). A Google search will also direct you accordingly.